Praise for *Experimenting with Kids*

"Observing children as they develop tells us so much about them—and even more about us as their parents. Whether you're a novice scientist or an experienced one, this book offers a meaningful and fascinating way to expand your abilities as a parent using the beauty of science!"

—MAYIM BIALIK, PHD, #1 NEW YORK TIMES BESTSELLING
AUTHOR OF GIRLING UP AND BEYOND THE SLING

"Now you can get into mischief before your child does! Shaun Gallagher takes a daring, whimsical approach to illuminating development in the most formative years. You'll get all caught up in the fun and games (a good thing!), and also learn a lot about your child. Truly, a top-notch approach to parent education."

—AUBREY HARGIS, AUTHOR OF TODDLER DISCIPLINE
FOR EVERY AGE AND STAGE

"So fun! But also important: The more you practice observing and guiding your child, the easier it will be to let go of hovering and controlling. Your child will thank you for doing these experiments."

—TRACY CUTCHLOW, AUTHOR OF ZERO TO FIVE: 70 ESSENTIAL
PARENTING TIPS BASED ON SCIENCE

D1303301

EXPERIMENTING WITH
KIDS

50 Amazing Science Projects

YOU CAN PERFORM ON YOUR CHILD AGES 2–5

SHAUN GALLAGHER

A TARCHERPERIGEE BOOK

An imprint of Penguin Random House LLC
penguinrandomhouse.com

TarcherPerigee with tp colophon is a registered trademark of Penguin Random House LLC.

Most TarcherPerigee books are available at special quantity discounts for bulk purchase for sales promotions, premiums, fund-raising, and educational needs. Special books or book excerpts also can be created to fit specific needs. For details, write: SpecialMarkets@penguinrandomhouse.com.

ISBN 9780143133551 (trade paperback)
ISBN 9780525505358 (ebook)

Printed in the United States of America
1   3   5   7   9   10   8   6   4   2

Book design by Ellen Cipriano

To my children

CONTENTS

Introduction

Your child has graduated from babyhood, and although life may have been easier during that wondrous time before he or she could talk back, scurry away, or draw on the furniture, the upside is that with each newfound ability your child develops, there are new opportunities to do science experiments.

In *Experimenting with Babies*, I presented fifty science projects that parents can perform on their kid, starting from birth and continuing to about twenty-four months. But the fun doesn't need to stop there. *Experimenting on Kids* covers the years from ages two to five, a time of rapid growth in many aspects of your child's development. It can also be a time of strong growth in your development as a parent. By learning more about what's going on in your child's adorable little head, you can then apply that knowledge in your everyday interactions to support your child's growth, which in turn can further cement the bond between you and your child.

Each of the fifty science projects presented here is adapted from published academic research in various fields of child development. The areas of research are varied—motor development, language development, cognitive development—and each of the projects can be performed using ordinary household objects, with no special equipment needed. None of the studies on which the projects are based are more than twenty years old, and about half of the studies were published within the past ten years.

Every project includes the following sections:

- **The experiment**, a set of instructions for how to perform it on your child

- **The hypothesis**, a prediction about what your child will do

- **The research**, a description of the study on which the experiment is based and its implications

- **The takeaway**, practical tips for parents on how to use the information you've learned to support and encourage your child and strengthen your parental bond

The projects are arranged so those that apply to younger children are toward the front and those that apply to older children are toward the back, but keep in mind that the age ranges are merely suggestions, and you do not need to do all of the projects in order. But you should try to set aside quality time for them. It might be helpful to read through the project instructions first, then plan to do the experiment at a time when neither you nor your child feels rushed, distracted, or cranky.

If your child struggles to accomplish any of the tasks laid out in the experiments or does not do what is predicted in the hypothesis, don't worry! It's perfectly normal for at least some of the participants in any study to respond differently than the majority, and the average age at which children reach developmental milestones or pick up new skills is just that—an average. Over the course of fifty projects, it would be surprising if your child *didn't* respond differently than predicted for a portion of them, so there's no need to push them to act in a certain way.

It is important that parents understand these science experiments are not intended to diagnose your child with any condition or show whether your child "measures up" to any standard. For that, please consult your pediatrician.

This book is also not intended to hasten any developmental milestone or make your child any smarter, stronger, or more adorable. In fact, if there's any overarching lesson parents should take away from these projects, it's how amazing your child already is, as is. It is impressive enough that these little creatures are capable of skills such as learning a new language, but they go well beyond that. They synthesize what they've learned and use it to create new, expressive turns of phrase. It's incredible!

Parents too often measure their own children against the children of their friends, neighbors, or colleagues. But these projects are intended to show you that your kid is amazing regardless of how he or she differs from other children. I hope they lead you to feel the same sense of awe that I feel, marveling at how complex young children's brains are, and how cool it is that we as parents get to witness them develop and grow. I've had the privilege of witnessing my own kids progress through this age range, and watching them pick up new skills, express themselves, and reason about the world has been an incredible joy. Think about the sense of wonder you feel when you stare at something remarkably small and intricate, like a cell under a microscope, or something unfathomably large and vast, like a supercluster of galaxies. That's the same sort of wonder I hope these projects inspire in you when you interact with your child.

Enjoy the experiments!

1 In the Groove

AGE RANGE: 2 to 3 years

RESEARCH AREAS: Motivation, creativity, music

 THE EXPERIMENT

Find a time when you can immerse yourself in an extended musical play session with your toddler (twenty minutes or more). Gather some common toys used in musical play, such as songbooks, recordings, a toy microphone, scarves, an egg shaker, a tambourine, or other small musical instruments. Allow your child to spontaneously direct the activities according to his interests. You might spend time manipulating the instruments, singing, dancing, or tapping along to recorded music, or looking at songbooks.

As you are playing with your child, look for signs that he is highly engaged and using his skills to the best of his ability. Indicators of this state, which some people describe as being "in the groove" or "in the zone," include:

- Purposefully initiating activities, rather than waiting for an adult to direct them
- Acknowledging and correcting errors, such as a wrong note or a jumbled lyric, without needing guidance from an adult
- Focused and controlled movements and gestures
- Indicating, verbally or physically, what happens next in an activity
- Completing a verse sung by an adult, or participating in call-and-response singing
- Making an activity more challenging by introducing some novel element, such as adding gestures or rhythmic clapping to a song
- Returning to a previous activity after some time has passed

 THE HYPOTHESIS

Your toddler is likely to be assertive in his preferences during this child-directed play period, selecting activities on his own and possibly remaining focused in them for extended periods. His hand and body movements will likely be deliberate and purposeful. If self-correction occurs, such as by misidentifying a musical instrument and then giving the correct name without prompting, it will probably be infrequent. He may also display anticipatory behavior, such as prematurely performing gestures that accompany a song. And he will probably both expand on activities, adding his own flourishes, and extend those activities, by humming a tune he had been singing earlier, for instance.

 THE RESEARCH

Music has an incredible ability to draw people—adults and children alike—into a state of *flow*, a term coined by famed Hungarian psychologist Mihaly Csikszentmihalyi to describe high engagement in an enjoyable and challenging activity. When you're in a state of flow, you feel not only happiness but also a sense of purpose and fulfillment. Time flies. You've found your groove.

A 2005 study sought to better understand how very young children enter a state of flow when engaged musically. The study's author, a music education researcher, spent time leading toddler music sessions, during which she presented the children with materials used in music play and allowed them to choose what engaged them.

She found that the children, who were between twenty-five and thirty-four months old, exhibited many behaviors that indicated a state of flow. They were highly engaged, often assertively self-initiated activities, and made deliberate, animated gestures, as when listening to recorded music. They showed signs of anticipation, such as beginning a certain song when its corresponding instrument was brought out; expansion, such as adding body movement to songs; and extension, such as humming a song that had previously been sung. This age group didn't, however, exhibit many self-correcting behaviors, which tend to indicate that the child is focused and has found a sweet spot between "too challenging" and "not challenging enough." Self-correction was, however, noticed among older, school-aged children who were also observed as part of the study, so it may be that this behavior emerges later in development than some of the other flow indicators.

 THE TAKEAWAY

You may have noticed that there are certain activities that your child can't seem to get enough of: reading and rereading a favorite book, singing along to an album, playing hide-and-seek, or playing pretend with a beloved toy. Although these activities may appear somewhat monotonous to you, they are your child's version of a jazz jam session. These activities engage and delight, allow him to exercise his brain without overwhelming him, and get him into his groove. If you are enjoying music or another favorite activity together and it seems like he's lost his groove, help him find it again by guiding him toward activities that are enriching and moderately challenging, and that are rewarding not only as a means to an end, but also for their own sake.

2 Impossible Adding

AGE RANGE: 2 to 3 years

RESEARCH AREAS: Number sense, agency

THE EXPERIMENT

You will need a cardboard box with an open bottom. Cut a hole in the side of the box that is large enough that you can reach inside to add or remove items. Then, cut a large flap in the front of the box, so that raising the flap reveals what has been placed in the box. You will also need three identical trinkets, such as Duplo bricks or green army men.

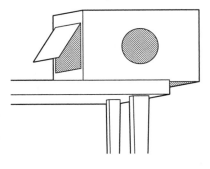

Place the cardboard box in front of you on a table so that it rests about an inch or two beyond the end of the table closest to you. Position the box so the side with the large flap is facing away from you. Place one of the trinkets inside the box, and have your child sit opposite you at the table, so the side with the flap is facing her. Lift up the flap and point out that there is one trinket inside the box. Then, lower the flap. Produce a second trinket and explain that you are going to place it inside the box. Reach into the hole in the side of the box and place the second trinket inside. Withdraw your hand, making sure that your child notices it is now empty. Then, reach into the hole again and remove one of the trinkets. At this point, surreptitiously place a trinket back into the box under the table through the open bottom. Then, open the front flap again to reveal the two trinkets. Ask your child, "Is that right? Should there be two trinkets?" Note her answer.

Next, repeat the demonstration. Begin again with one trinket. Add one to the box, then subtract one from the box. This time, don't surreptitiously add a trinket. Lift the front flap again to reveal the single trinket. Ask your child, "Is that right? Should there be one trinket?" Note her answer.

About a week later, repeat the two demonstrations again, with one change: instead of manipulating the trinkets yourself, direct your child to add and remove the trinkets via the hole in the side of the box.

THE HYPOTHESIS

When you are the one who adds and removes the trinkets from the box, your child may have difficulty identifying whether there should be one or two trinkets left in the box at the end of each demonstration. But when your child is the one who manipulates the trinkets, she is likely to be able to accurately say whether there should be one or two trinkets remaining.

THE RESEARCH

In a 2015 study, two-year-old children were assigned to one of two groups. Both groups were shown a box similar to the one you used in your experiment. In the "onlookers" group, the experimenter was the one who added and removed toys from the box. In the "actors" group, the child was the one who added and removed the toys.

In some cases, the number of toys inside the box was not manipulated, but in other cases, the researchers manipulated the number of toys inside the box to cause an impossible outcome. In one instance, the experiment began with one toy inside the box. After the front of the box was closed, a toy was added, then a toy was removed. A toy was then surreptitiously added, and when the contents were revealed, the child saw that there were two toys inside. The child was then prompted to say whether the outcome was correct or incorrect.

The researchers found that in the onlookers group, the children's ability to answer correctly did not differ from chance. They were just as likely to say that the result was correct as they were to say that it was incorrect. However, in the actors group, the children gave the correct answer about 85 percent of the time.

The type of arithmetical operation depicted in the experiment is called an inversion problem, because it illustrates the inversion principle between addition and subtraction. When you add a certain number of items to a group, and then subtract the same number of items, the subtraction operation reverses, or inverts, the addition operation. The researchers found that when it comes to basic arithmetical operations, young children have a special aptitude for inversion problems. In related experiments, they found that the children had more difficulty with similar operations that did not involve inversion.

THE TAKEAWAY

Manipulating the materials does not make your child any smarter. Rather, self-action, which involves active participation rather than passive observation, appears to bring out your child's natural potential. As a parent, look out for other ways in which your child can tap into intrinsic knowledge by manipulating the world around her. For instance, she might have a rudimentary understanding of how a mechanical toy works, and when you demonstrate its functionality, it may help her pick up a few points. But there's nothing quite like hands-on play to help her understand the ins and outs of how it works. With abstract concepts such as addition and subtraction, finding ways for your child to exercise her brain through physical manipulation of objects can be especially helpful. For young children, the best way to pick up new understanding might be to pick up new objects.

③ Syntactic Sugar

AGE RANGE: 2 to 3 years
RESEARCH AREA: Language development

 THE EXPERIMENT

Recruit a partner to help conduct the experiment. Allow your child to watch you and your partner as you look at the first pair of illustrations, which depict a woman tickling a baby and a woman clapping her hands. Show these illustrations to your child, then say to your partner, "Look! The woman is tickling the baby." Your partner should respond, "Wow, the woman *is* tickling the baby!" Next, show your child the first pair of illustrations again. Say, "Find tickling," and prompt your child to point to a picture. Note which illustration he points to.

Next, you and your partner should look at the second pair

of illustrations, which depict a man holding a child and a man bending at the waist. Say to your partner, "Look! The man is bending." Your partner should respond, "That's right, the

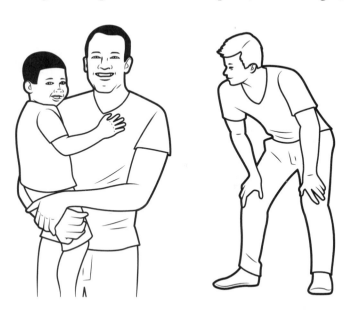

man *is* bending." Then show your child the second pair of illustrations. Say, "Find bending," and again prompt your child to point to a picture. Note which illustration he points to.

Finally, you and your partner should look at the third pair of illustrations, which depict two novel actions. In one, a woman holds the outstretched leg of a man seated in a chair, and in the other, a man holds one arm in the air in a Statue of Liberty pose. Say to your partner, "Look, this person is gorping." Your partner should respond, "Yes, I see. The person *is* gorping." Now, show the third pair of illustrations to your child and say, "Find gorping." Prompt him to point to an illustration, and note which one he points to.

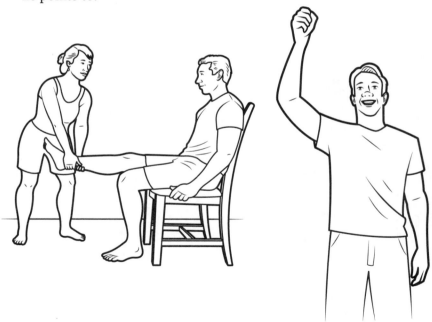

THE HYPOTHESIS

When you ask your child to find "gorping," he will point to the picture of the man holding one arm in the air and will look longer at it than at the other picture.

THE RESEARCH

Children don't usually learn new verbs in isolation. They hear the verbs used in sentences, and the structure of the sentences gives clues to the verb's meaning. For instance, a sentence might be transitive or intransitive. In a transitive sentence, which contains a subject, a verb, and a direct object, the subject is doing something to someone or something else. ("The woman tickles the baby" is a transitive sentence.) In an intransitive sentence, which has a subject and a verb but no direct object, the subject is doing something—but the action is not being done to someone or something else. ("The man bends" is an intransitive sentence.)

Researchers in a 2009 study were curious about whether two-year-old children are able to pick up on these syntactic clues when they hear an unfamiliar verb and use those clues to figure out what the verb might mean. In one experiment, children first listened to dialogues in which a familiar verb (such as *tickle* or *bend*) was used. They were then shown two scenes. One depicted the familiar verb being demonstrated, and the other depicted a different verb. The children were then asked to identify which picture represented the familiar verb they had heard in the dialogue.

Then, children listened to dialogues containing a nonsense verb (such as *blick* or *gorp*). In some cases, the dialogues used the nonsense verb in a transitive sentence, and in other cases, the dialogues used it in an intransitive sentence. The children were then shown two scenes. One depicted a transitive action, in which a person was doing something to another person. The other depicted an intransitive action, in which a single person was shown performing the act. The children were asked to look at the picture that represented the nonsense verb they had heard in the dialogue, and the amount of time they looked at the image was recorded.

The researchers found that children who had heard the nonsense verb used in a transitive sentence looked longer at the picture with two people in it, and children who'd heard it used in an intransitive sentence looked longer at the picture with one person in it. That's why your child is likely to have associated "gorping" with the picture of the man holding one arm in the air—because "He is gorping" is an intransitive sentence, and the picture depicts an intransitive action.

These results suggest that children as young as two years old can deduce meaningful information from the structure of the sentence in which a novel verb is used, and they can later use that information to determine what the verb might mean.

THE TAKEAWAY

Your child may not even be able to say "parts of speech," let alone understand what the phrase means, but the ability to extract information from the syntax of a sentence and use it to determine the meaning of novel words appears to be present even before he has acquired the ability to put together complex sentences on his own. As a parent, understanding that your baby's brain works this way takes the pressure off a bit. You don't have to buy flash cards or fancy apps to help your baby learn language. He's picking up words and meanings just by listening to everyday conversation. What you *can* do to help him learn is give him opportunities to listen to that conversation. You might, for instance, narrate your actions as you go about your daily tasks, which can help him pick up both vocabulary and grammar. And, perhaps more important, you should converse with him directly, giving him opportunities to respond, inquire, or otherwise interact with you.

The 30-Million-Word Gap

In 1995, educational researchers Betty Hart and Todd Risley published a book that asserts there is an enormous "word gap" between children born to low-income families and children born to affluent, white-collar families. They wrote that by the end of their preschool years, children in low-income families hear about thirty million fewer words spoken by caregivers than children in affluent families, and the researchers linked this to a difference in child outcomes in various measurements of academic achievement a few years later. Their work on the word gap has been highly cited, but it hasn't gone unchallenged.

In a 2019 study, child development researchers examined historical language data and conducted home visits to observe children interacting with caregivers. They found that the amount of spoken language within and across socioeconomic classes varies widely, and that when overheard speech (rather than just direct conversations between caregiver and child) is accounted for, the word gap essentially disappears.

However, a critique of this study published later in 2019 noted that not all overheard speech is of the same quality. In experiments such as the one you conducted in the preceding project, children are able to be fully attentive to the overheard speech, but in real life, they are often eavesdropping on parents' conversations while the majority of their attention is focused on something else. Its authors conclude: "Overhearing language about death and taxes—topics of interest to adults—can never be as effective for language learning as participating in contingent conversations about what matters to children." They insist that even if the word gap is smaller than initially thought, it's the quality of the conversation, rather than the mere number of words heard, that is the factor most likely to influence children's future performance. In other words, your child is absorbing language every time he hears it, but taking the time to engage with him directly, narrating as you go, is well worth the effort.

4 Artistic Intent

AGE RANGE: 2 to 3 years

RESEARCH AREA: Perception

 THE EXPERIMENT

You will need one medium-sized cardboard box that has an open top, and an opaque box of the same size that has a lid. You will also need two relatively flat, circular objects that your child is not familiar with, such as a sink strainer and a collapsible cup. Finally, gather a clipboard or other portable writing surface, a piece of paper, and a drawing instrument, such as a marker or crayon.

Seat your child at a table with the open-top box to her left and the box with the lid to her right. Show the insides of the boxes to your child to demonstrate that they are empty. Next, give the two novel objects to your child and allow her to explore them for a few moments. Then, place one of the objects inside the open-top box, so that she is no longer able to see the object. Place the other object inside the other box and close the lid. Place your paper on the clipboard and stand in such a way that your child can clearly see you looking into the open box. Spend about five seconds drawing a circular shape as you refer back to the open box.

Now, place your completed drawing in the center of the table. Remove the two objects from the boxes and place them to the left and right of the drawing. Say to your child, "Look! A zerbit! I drew a zerbit. See the zerbit!" Finally, prompt your child to point to a zerbit.

 THE HYPOTHESIS

There are three possible objects your child might point to: the object that was in the open-top box, the paper with your drawing, or the object that was in the box with the closed lid. Your child is twice as likely to point to the object that was in the open-top box than to point to the drawing, and not likely at all to point to the object that was in the box with the closed lid.

 THE RESEARCH

In a 2002 study, children were shown a drawing that looked like a fish, but they were told that the artist who drew the picture came from a faraway place where there were no fish. Nevertheless, when the children were asked what the drawing depicted, children under age eight tended to say that it was a fish, while children eight and older tended to realize that since the artist did not know what a fish was, she could not have intended for it to depict a fish.

Researchers in a 2008 study wanted to explore whether a simpler, more direct way to communicate artistic intent—gazing at an object while drawing—could show whether children as young as two years old might be capable of taking into account an artist's intent to infer what a drawing is meant to represent. Each child participated in two trials, during which they saw a presentation much like the one you did with your child. In one of the trials, the adult experimenter peered into the open-top box while drawing a shape. In the other trial, the adult peered at the wall behind the box with the closed lid. At the end of each trial, the children were prompted to point to the object that had been labeled with a nonsense word.

The researchers found that in the trials where the experimenter peered into the open-top box while drawing, about 60 percent of children pointed to the novel object that had been inside that box, about 25 percent pointed to the drawing, and about 15 percent pointed to the other novel object. However, in trials where the experimenter looked at the wall behind the box with the closed lid, the children were just about equally likely to point at either the drawing or the object that had been in the box with the closed lid. Only about 10 percent of children pointed to the novel object that had been in the open-top box.

These results suggest that children as young as two are indeed capable of understanding that drawings often are meant to depict real-world objects, and of taking into account an artist's gaze toward an object to infer what a particular drawing represents.

THE TAKEAWAY

At the ripe old age of two, your child has already come to a rudimentary understanding of a basic principle of art: intent matters. Of course, later on she might insist that a painting of a fish is a painting of a fish no matter what the artist intended. But for right now, understanding an artist's intention will help her make sense of the world. That doesn't mean, however, that your child is always able to pick up on subtle contextual clues, so when you are exposing her to art in its many forms, try to give her direct information about its backstory. For younger kids, explain any unfamiliar words or images depicted and talk a little bit about authors, musicians, and artists they encounter. For older kids, address questions such as: Why did the composer create this symphony? What story is this ballet depicting through dance? How does this sculpture fit into its creator's body of work? How can we know that? Doing so will help them better understand and appreciate what motivates other people to make art, and it may also motivate them to make their own art as well.

⑤ Sticking Around

AGE RANGE: 2 to 3 years

RESEARCH AREAS: Cognitive development, motor skills

 THE EXPERIMENT

For this experiment, you'll need a small toy, such as a plastic fig-urine, and a straight stick, wooden dowel, or other similar rigid object that your child can grasp and use to push the toy. You'll also need a small piece of blue construction paper, about five inches by five inches.

At one end of a medium-sized table, center the toy.

Have your child stand at the other end of the table. (It might be useful to have him stand on a small stool so that he is less likely to move from his designated spot.)

If your child is left-handed, tape the piece of construction paper on the right-hand corner of the table on the side closest to him. If he's right-handed, or if you're not quite sure what his dominant hand is, tape the construction paper on the left-hand corner of the table.

Then, place the stick in the middle of the table so it divides the table into a "toy side" and a "child side."

To begin the experiment, tell your child that the blue construction paper represents a bathtub, and the toy needs a bath, but it needs help getting into the tub. Direct your child to pick up the stick and use it to move the toy onto the construction-paper bathtub. Try not to give any hints about how he should accomplish this task, but feel free to give general encouragement.

As he performs the task, make note of which hand he uses to grasp the stick and whether he switches hands while trying to push the toy onto the construction paper.

Once he has completed the task, switch the construction paper to the other corner (still on the same side of the table as your child) and repeat the experiment. If you are performing this project with a two-year-old, try it again a year later to see what's changed.

 THE HYPOTHESIS

At two years old, your child is very likely to use his dominant hand (which is probably his right hand) to both grasp the stick and use it to move the toy, regardless of whether the construction-paper bathtub is to the left or right of him. If he does use his nondominant hand to grasp, he may switch to his dominant hand at some point in the process. At three years old, he is more likely to use his left hand when the construction paper is to the right of him and his right hand when the paper is to the left of him, although his hand preference may also have some influence.

 THE RESEARCH

In a 2006 study, a group of two-year-olds and a group of three-year-olds participated in an experiment similar to the one you just did. The researchers found that children in the two groups reached for the stick in markedly different ways.

Roughly three-quarters of the two-year-olds used their right hand to grasp the stick, and some who had initially used their left hand to grasp it switched to their right hand to move the toy. Whether the "bathtub" goal was to the left or to the right of the child didn't make much difference.

In contrast, the three-year-olds behaved differently depending on whether the goal was to their left or to their right. If it was to the left, 95 percent grasped and moved the stick using their right hand. If it was to the right, only about half used their right hand. The results also showed that the three-year-olds switched hands during the task less than the two-year-olds did.

What explains the difference in results between the two age groups?

The researchers think it's likely that goal-related information influenced the older children's behavior, but not the younger children's. The three-year-olds essentially planned out the task in their heads and realized that it is easier to move the toy to the goal using a sweeping motion, which can be accomplished by grasping the stick with the hand that is not on the same side as the goal. (Obviously, hand preference also influenced the children's decision, since half of the three-year-olds still used their right hand even when it would have made more sense to use their left.)

The behavior exhibited by the two-year-olds suggests that only hand preference influenced their choices, not any sort of action planning. In fact, because hand switching, when it occurred, tended to be from the left hand to the right, it suggests that hand preference strongly influenced not only the initial grasping decision but also the decision about how to actually transport the toy. The researchers think this is because using the stick to move the toy is a more demanding task than simply grasping the stick, so the children switched to their more dexterous right hand, valuing a higher degree of motor control over efficiency of movement.

THE TAKEAWAY

You might be familiar with auto racing arcade games in which you can choose between a fast car that handles well or a faster car that is harder to control. Which one would you choose? At two years old, your child is faced with a similar choice, particularly if he already has a clearly dominant hand. He knows he can handle that dominant hand better, and so on a daunting task, having extra control is more of a priority than speed. At three years old, however, two things have changed: he's gained more control over both his dominant and nondominant sides, and he's made strides in his cognitive development, so the task may seem less daunting.

Now that you know a bit about how these factors shape your child's behavior, use that knowledge to help guide your interactions with him. For instance, if your two-year-old is a right-hander, you might want to place his fork to the right of his plate, since he'll likely be using his right hand to grab it no matter where you put it and you'd rather he not get his elbows in his food. But as your child gets older, feel free to follow Emily Post's rules of table etiquette and place the fork to the left; he'll figure out an efficient way to grasp the utensil and pass it to his dominant hand.

6 Winners, More or Less

AGE RANGE: 2 to 3 years

RESEARCH AREA: Cognitive development

 THE EXPERIMENT

First, gather your materials. You'll need six Dixie cups (or other small containers), two trays or plates that can each hold five of the cups, and a few sheets of stickers to use as prizes.

Begin by placing one of the cups upside down on one tray. On the other tray, place two of the cups upside down and hide a sticker under each of them.

Show each tray to your child, side by side. Then pick up the single cup on the first tray and reveal that there is nothing under it. Say, "Look, this is the loser. There's nothing inside." Next, pick up both cups on the second tray and reveal the stickers. Say,

"Look, this is the winner, and the stickers are for you." Now switch the position of the trays and point out that even though the trays are in different positions, the tray with two cups remains the winner and the tray with one cup remains the loser.

Now restock the stickers on the tray with two cups and ask your child to point to the winner. If she chooses correctly, allow her to retrieve the stickers from under the cups. If she chooses incorrectly, prompt her to choose again, and then let her retrieve the stickers from under the cups.

After a few rounds of this, it's time to vary the number of cups on each tray. You might, for instance, try one cup on one tray and three cups on the other; two cups on one tray and four cups on the other; or one cup on one tray and five cups on the other. In each case, the tray with the greater number of cups on it should have stickers under each cup and should be treated as the winner. Continue to prompt your child to choose the winner.

 THE HYPOTHESIS

Your child will quickly catch on that the winner is the tray with more cups on it, even if you never use the words *greater*, *more*, *fewer*, or *less*. She will probably do best when the comparison is between one and two cups, but she may also do well when you vary the number of cups.

THE RESEARCH

Researchers in a 2001 study conducted a series of experiments involving two- and three-year-olds to determine their number competence, and specifically to determine if they could infer, without being explicitly told, the rule that determined which tray was the winner, and then generalize that rule.

In one of the experiments, which involved only two-year-olds, the participants went through a series of tasks like those described here, only instead of Dixie cups the researchers used small red boxes. In the one-box versus two-box condition, children correctly chose the winner about 75 percent of the time. That's a lot more than one would expect if they were just choosing at random, so it certainly seems as if they inferred some sort of rule.

But what rule? It couldn't have been a position-based rule, because sometimes the winner was the tray on the left and sometimes it was the tray on the right. Maybe, though, the rule they learned was "The winner is whichever tray has exactly two boxes on it." To rule that out, they looked at how the children performed when the number of boxes was changed. It turns out that they still performed better than chance, even in a condition involving nine boxes total (four versus five boxes), although never quite as well as with the one-box versus two-box condition.

It appears, based on these results, that the children were able to infer the "greater than" versus "less than" rule and apply it to groupings beyond what had been demonstrated.

But how did they figure out which tray had the greater number of containers?

You might think they counted them, but although two-year-olds often can recite a short counting sequence, they tend not to be able to understand how the sequence actually relates to numerosity. In other words, even if they are able to count to five, and even if they are able to point to objects as they recite the sequence, there's still a further mental leap required to arrive at "I've counted to five, and that means there are five objects here." Consistent with this, none of the two-year-olds in the study used number words or were observed counting the containers one by one.

So, if counting doesn't explain it, what does?

One possibility is that they simply observed which tray had more of its surface area covered in containers. The researchers ran a subsequent experiment in which the size of the containers varied, but two large containers still lost out against three small containers. The children still inferred the greater-than/less-than rule, which supports the idea that they weren't simply using surface area to make their comparison.

The researchers concluded that children as young as two years old are able to make ordinal comparisons without explicitly counting because they are able to mentally grasp the concept of numerosity, even if they haven't yet tied that concept to counting or number words.

In the field of machine learning, which is enjoying its heyday after a long period of relatively modest advances, teaching a computer to make even simple inferences about unstated game rules can be challenging. Fortunately, your toddler's brain is able to pick up on these rules with no programming involved! (Don't be discouraged, however, if she didn't get all the trials right. Children in the original study picked the winner only 60 percent of the time when presented with novel number pairings.)

There are at least two practical lessons to glean from this research. The first is that at two years old, your child is already picking up on rules, even those that aren't clearly spelled out, so now's a great time to introduce her to simple games and puzzles. The second lesson is that if you want to motivate a two-year-old to be your science project, stickers are a terrific incentive!

Preschool Pain Scales

Can preschoolers' numerical literacy predict how accurately they are able to self-report pain? It's a question pain researchers would like to answer, because knowing whether a child's self-reports are accurate can help doctors and other health care workers better address and manage that pain.

A 2011 study gave several screening tasks to preschoolers who were about to have outpatient surgery, including tasks related to numerical literacy. Although several of the screening

tasks did help predict self-reported pain accuracy, none was any better as a screening tool than chronological age.

However, that doesn't mean there are no opportunities to improve the way children are asked to rate their pain. One standard pain scale used with preschool-aged children shows six illustrations of faces whose expressions correspond to a pain scale of 0 to 10. But a 2013 study found improved results among preschoolers with a two-step simplified pain assessment. First, the child is asked, "Does it hurt?" And if she responds yes, she's shown just three faces, representing no pain, moderate pain, and severe pain. Five-year-old children who viewed picture stories depicting painful events were able to give pain ratings with roughly the same accuracy regardless of whether they used the standard or the simplified rating system. But among three- and four-year-old participants, accuracy was higher when using the simplified rating system. If you'd like to try this with your own child, use the three-face test shown here the next time she takes a spill.

Bad Liars

AGE RANGE: 2 to 3 years

RESEARCH AREAS: Cognitive development, deception, executive function

THE EXPERIMENT

You'll need to gather three different animal toys, such as a cat, a pig, and a duck. For each animal, your child should be able to correctly answer the question "What sound does this animal make?" You'll also need a cloth or other covering that you can place over the animals to obscure them from view. Finally, you'll need to set up an unobtrusive camera, such as those used in baby monitors, that can be used to surreptitiously record your child during the experiment.

Direct your child to sit down in the center of a room. Explain that you are going to play a game that involves guessing animal noises. Tell him that you are going to place a toy animal behind him, out of his view, and he should remain facing forward so that he cannot see the toy. You will imitate the sound the animal makes, and your child should try to guess what animal it is. Once he guesses correctly, direct him to turn around and see the toy animal. Do this for the first two animals.

For the third animal, place the toy, uncovered, behind him, but then explain that before continuing, you need to retrieve something, and he should sit facing forward and not turn around. Go to an area of the room where you are within his line of sight, turn your back toward him, and rummage around for about one minute to find an item. (For instance, you might look through a bookshelf and eventually produce a storybook that contains animals.) Walk behind your child and cover the third toy with the cloth.

Now ask your child, "While I had my back turned to you, did you peek at the toy?" Make note of whether your child confesses. Then ask, "What animal do you think it is?" and note your child's answer.

 THE HYPOTHESIS

When you review the video, you are likely to find that your child peeked, although the likelihood decreases with age. If your child did indeed peek, his age probably also predicts whether he admitted doing so. Younger two-year-olds are likely to admit it, while older three-year-olds are unlikely to admit it. If your child lies about having peeked, he is likely to be unable to maintain the lie. When you ask him what animal he thinks it is, he is likely to answer with the correct animal name, even though he ostensibly should not know it.

 THE RESEARCH

Researchers in a 2013 study were interested in how young children are when they first begin lying. They played a guessing game with two- and three-year-olds, similar to the game that you played with your child, and observed whether the child peeked while the adult experimenter's back was turned. Practically all of the younger two-year-olds peeked. The likelihood of peeking decreased with age, although even with older three-year-olds, more than 60 percent peeked. Among the children who peeked, their age predicted whether they would lie about having done so. Among the younger children, a large majority fessed up, but among the older group of participants, 90 percent lied. However, few children who lied were able to maintain the lie. When they were asked which animal they thought was behind them, about three-quarters of the children blurted out the name of the animal.

Also as part of the study, the experimenters tested the children on executive functions, which are cognitive processes that help us follow instructions, plan and organize, and exhibit self-control. They found that children who performed better on these tasks were more likely to lie. This stands to reason, because children tend to be impulsive truth tellers (sometimes inconveniently so), and the ability to inhibit this impulse makes it possible for them to lie.

 THE TAKEAWAY

You're probably thinking: Okay, I've demonstrated that my kid is capable of lying to me. But how do I get him to tell the truth?

Science to the rescue! A 2018 study of three- and four-year-olds involved a similar command to not peek at a toy. As expected, many of the children did peek. The researchers found that having children promise to tell the truth about whether they peeked did not significantly affect the honesty of their response, compared with a control group. But one other strategy did have an effect. The researchers had the child look at himself or herself in the mirror for a short time before giving an answer, which the researchers called the "self-awareness" condition. Children in this group were significantly more likely to tell the truth, compared with the control group.

So, the next time someone swipes a cookie from the cookie jar, try to instill a sense of self-awareness by giving him some time to reflect—in the closest mirror.

8 Success Is Successive

AGE RANGE: 2 to 3 years

RESEARCH AREA: Language development

 THE EXPERIMENT

This experiment has two parts, which can be done at separate times.

For part one, refer to the three illustrations on page 242. Each depicts a made-up object, and each is labeled with a nonsense word. You will show these images to your child one at a time, so use scrap paper to cover up the other two images when they're not needed.

Show your child the first image, labeled "trep." Say, "Do you know what a trep is? Wow, this trep looks cool! Do you see the trep there?" Next, show your child the second image, labeled "daro." Say, "Do you know what a daro is? Wow, this daro looks cool! Do you see the daro there?" Then, show your child the third image, labeled "bax." Say, "Do you know what a bax is? Wow, this bax looks cool! Do you see the bax there?"

Next, turn to page 244 and show your child the top two images. Say, "Where is the trep? Do you see it?" Prompt her to point to the trep, and note which of the images she points to.

In the second part of the experiment, which you can do at a later time, refer to the three illustrations on page 243. Again, you will show these images to your child one at a time, but this time, instead of showing each image and reciting a block of sentences, you are going to chop things up, cycling through the images as you speak each sentence.

Show the first image, labeled "bram," and say, "Do you know what a bram is?" Then show the second image, labeled "pelk," and say, "Wow, this pelk looks cool!" Then show the third image, labeled "troom," and say, "Do you see the troom there?"

Next, show the second image and say, "Do you know what a pelk is?" Then show the third image and say, "Wow, this troom looks cool!" Then show the first image and say, "Do you see the bram there?"

Next, show the third image and say, "Do you know what a troom is?" Then show the first image and say, "Wow, this bram looks cool!" Then show the second image and say, "Do you see the pelk there?"

Finally, turn to page 244 and show your child the bottom two images. Say, "Where is the troom? Do you see it?" Prompt her to point to the troom, and note which of the images she points to.

 THE HYPOTHESIS

Your child is more likely to point to the correct image in the first part of the experiment than in the second part.

 THE RESEARCH

Children in a 2016 study were split into two groups. In one group, the children were shown pictures of made-up objects with non-sense labels while blocks of sentences that referred to the objects were spoken. In the other group, the same sentences were used to refer to the same objects, but they were ordered in such a way that no adjacent sentences referred to the same object.

The results revealed that the children's ability to correctly identify the target image was greater than chance only in the group that heard the blocks of sentences. The children in the other group were just as often incorrect as they were correct.

Because the children in both groups heard the words with the same frequency, the researchers concluded that the difference in performance points to another important aspect of language acquisition during early childhood: repetition. In particular, children appear to learn words more easily, and demonstrate short-term retention of those words, when they are repeated multiple times within a short time frame, with few distractions or interruptions. That said, an earlier study found that repetition over longer periods of time can help with long-term retention.

 **THE TAKEAWAY**

Perhaps you can empathize with your child. If you have ever tried to balance a checkbook while also preparing dinner and keeping an eye on the baby monitor, you probably know that multitasking is, well, no easy task. Being able to focus intently on one thing at a time can help you avoid mistakes, and it can help your child with all sorts of learning tasks, language acquisition among them. So look for opportunities for undistracted, uninterrupted learning. If you know that your child is least distractible after a good nap, try to set aside that time to introduce new concepts and build in repetition to help her catch on.

The Long and the Short

AGE RANGE: 2 to 3 years

RESEARCH AREA: Perception

 THE EXPERIMENT

Prior to a mealtime, select two similar-sized rod-shaped food items that you know your child will desire, such as two pretzel sticks. You'll also need a piece of dark construction paper. From one of the sticks, break off about one-third and consume it yourself. Position the two sticks on the table and have your child sit down. Explain to your child that in a moment, he will have an opportunity to select either the larger or the smaller pretzel stick to eat. Then, cover the two sticks with the construction paper and leave a portion of each stick uncovered, so that about three inches of the shorter stick and two inches of the longer stick are visible. Then prompt your child to point to the pretzel stick he wishes to eat.

THE HYPOTHESIS

Your child will select the bigger pretzel stick, even though at the time of selection it has been partially obscured in such a way that it appears to be the smaller of the two choices.

THE RESEARCH

In child-development studies, children who participate in an experiment are typically compared with other children. But in a 2014 study, human kids were pitted against other primates in an interspecies matchup.

The researchers conducted an experiment similar to the one you just conducted with your own child, in which pretzel sticks were obscured in a way that made their sizes appear to be the opposite of what they actually were. They found that in all the great ape species they tested—bonobos, chimpanzees, gorillas, and orangutans—as well as in two-and-a-half-year-old human children, the participants were much more likely to select the snack stick that was actually bigger.

The results offer evidence of a perceptual skill that appears to be present in early childhood and that also extends to our hairier cousins: the ability to make distinctions between appearance and reality.

THE TAKEAWAY

Picking the correct pretzel in the preceding experiment involves a bunch of work inside your child's brain. For instance, he must remember the sizes of the pretzel sticks even after they are obscured, and he must overcome an impulsive attraction to the pretzel that appears to be the larger one at the time of selection. That's hard work, and it will take quite a while for him to pick up on more subtle distinctions between appearance and reality. For instance, he might have a hard time understanding that a street performer in a scary-looking costume is actually a sweet person who loves interacting with kids. So, when you notice that your child is struggling with the appearance-reality distinction, feel free to step in and clear things up.

⑩ Wake or Sleep

AGE RANGE: 2 to 3 years

RESEARCH AREAS: Perception, social development

 THE EXPERIMENT

Either alone or with your child, you will assemble two shakers. You'll need two clear jars. The first jar will be the "quiet" shaker, so fill it with material such as glitter, sand, or sugar. The second jar will be the "loud" shaker, so fill it with material such as dried beans, marbles, or plastic beads.

Place lids on both jars and allow your child to manipulate them and observe the sounds they make when shaken. After a period of exploration, step out of the room briefly, and return cradling a doll in your arms. Explain that the doll is sleeping and that you don't want to wake him up. Then, point to the two shakers and ask your child which she wants to play with. Observe which object she chooses and note the volume of the sounds she makes (both her own vocalizations and the sounds she makes with the shaker). About a minute later, step out of the room briefly again, and return with the doll. Explain that now it's time for the doll to wake up. Then, point to the two shakers and ask your child which she wants to play with. Again, observe which object she chooses and note the volume of the sounds she makes.

 THE HYPOTHESIS

Your child is likely to decrease the intensity of the sounds she makes during the "don't wake" portion of the experiment and increase the intensity during the "wake" portion. Also, she is more likely to choose the loud shaker than the quiet shaker during the "wake" condition.

 THE RESEARCH

It's one thing to understand the difference between loud and soft. Even infants seem to be able to make that distinction. But it's a trickier skill to be able to understand how the sounds we make affect others, and to purposefully choose a volume level appropriate for a social task. In a 2015 study, researchers introduced children to novel toys that made either soft or loud sounds when shaken. The children were given an opportunity to play with each of them, and a short sound recording was made while they did so. Then an experimenter brought out a baby doll and said the doll was sleeping. One group of children was told not to wake the doll, and another group was told it was time to wake the baby. They were then given the opportunity to select one of the two toys. The researchers noted which toy was chosen and made a ten-second sound recording, starting from when the child touched the toy he or she selected. The sound recordings from both the familiarization phase and the test phase were then analyzed to determine the loudness of the child's actions, including sounds made using the shaker and any vocalizations or other sounds made by the child.

The researchers found that only in the "wake" condition were children significantly more likely to choose the loud shaker; the children in the "don't wake" condition were only slightly more likely to choose the quiet shaker. Nevertheless, the sounds they made with their selected toy were quite different between groups. Children in the "wake" condition made significantly louder sounds during the test phase than they did during the familiarization phase, suggesting that they purposefully got louder in order to wake the doll. Children in the "don't wake" condition, on the other hand, significantly decreased their volume during the test phase, compared with the familiarization phase, suggesting that they purposefully grew quieter in order to avoid waking the doll.

A further analysis revealed that the children's ability to appropriately modulate their sound according to a goal ("wake" or "don't wake") largely depended on whether the child had any siblings. Among participants with at least one sibling, sound intensity grew louder in the "wake" condition and quieter in the "don't wake" condition. But among participants with no siblings, there was no significant difference between their volume in the familiarization phase and the test phase, regardless of which condition they were in. The researchers think that having a sibling gives young children more opportunities to learn that making loud sounds is likely to wake others who are sleeping and making quiet sounds helps prevent disturbing them.

 **THE TAKEAWAY**

Determining the level of sound intensity that is appropriate for a particular social situation can be difficult for young children, and it should come as no surprise that they tend toward louder rather than quieter. Try to first work on the most basic distinction possible: "inside voice" versus "outside voice." You can then make more subtle distinctions, such as "When someone is sleeping, we use an inside voice that is barely above a whisper." If your child has already acquired the habit of using an outside voice when an inside voice is more appropriate, explain that you will not respond to a yelling voice and give her an opportunity to address you again in a quieter voice. This technique might not produce immediate results, but it will help her gradually understand that she needs to keep her volume under control.

11 That's the Point

AGE RANGE: 2 to 4 years

RESEARCH AREA: Memory and attention

 THE EXPERIMENT

For this experiment, you'll need a small stuffed animal, three identical containers that are large enough to fit the stuffed animal inside, a piece of candy or a sticker to use as a prize, and a camera or video monitor that can be used to record your child during the experiment.

Seat your child in a high chair, booster seat, or chair at a table. On the opposite end of the table, out of his reach, place the three containers upside down. Introduce the stuffed animal and explain that it is going to hold the candy and take a short rest inside one of the containers. Tell your child that you need to leave the room for a minute, and when you return, you will allow him to open one container. If he finds the stuffed animal under his chosen container, he will get the candy as a prize.

Leave the room for about one minute, and when you return, prompt him to lift the correct container. Make note of whether he successfully identifies the container with the stuffed animal and candy inside.

Either immediately afterward or at some later time, repeat the experiment once or twice more, and again note whether he chooses the correct container in each trial.

Later, review the video recordings of your child during the times you were not in the room. Make note of whether he uses a pointed finger in each trial to help him remember the location of the container with the stuffed animal. (If he takes any subversive measures, like peeking or removing the prize while you are out of the room, try the experiment again some other time.)

 THE HYPOTHESIS

The older your child is, the less likely he is to use a pointed finger as a memory aid, but the more likely he is to select the correct container. However, if your child uses a pointed finger in one trial but not another, his chances of identifying the correct container are greater when the pointed finger is used.

Children in a 2011 study were split into two groups. In one group, called the "remembering" condition, the children were told that the experimenter needed to leave the room for a minute, and if they remembered which of three containers held a teddy bear, they would receive candy as a prize. In the other group, called the "waiting" condition, the teddy bear was placed under the container, but the children were not prompted to remember its location or offered a prize for doing so.

The results showed that more than half the children in the "remembering" condition used a pointed finger in at least one trial, whereas very few children in the "waiting" condition did so, which suggests that in this context, pointing at an object tends to be done as a memory aid, not merely as a spontaneous action.

Surprisingly, children in the "remembering" group who used a pointed finger in at least some trials showed a poorer overall performance than children who did not point in any trials. The researchers noted that the kids who used a pointed finger tended to be on the younger side, and they reasoned that if memory power increases with age, it may be the case that older children both remember better and need fewer memory aids.

 **THE TAKEAWAY**

As a parent, you might think that when your child ceases to use a tool that had been helpful to him in the past, his performance on a given task will dip. But keep in mind that between ages two and four, children are still rapidly developing their existing skills, and just as a snake sheds its skin when it outgrows it, your child may cast off tools that had previously come in handy but that are no longer necessary or might even be holding him back. Don't be surprised, then, if there comes a time when taking off the training wheels of a bike allows your child to become a better cyclist, when graduating to a bowling lane without bumpers helps him become a better bowler, or when making the leap from finger counting to mental math allows him to make progress with arithmetic. Crutches can speed you up when you need them, but they can also slow you down when you don't, so give your child opportunities and encouragement to explore the world without them.

12 Leading Notes

AGE RANGE: 2 to 4 years

RESEARCH AREAS: Motivation, music

 THE EXPERIMENT

Set aside fifteen to twenty minutes during which your child can freely engage in musical play. This play can incorporate a number of musical elements. For instance, for part of the time you might play prerecorded music that encourages movement or dancing. For another part, you might offer instruments or toys that she can use to produce music. Allow your child to take the lead in determining which musical activities to engage in, and actively join in the play if she invites you to. Once your music play has finished, jot down some notes about how engaged your child was with the play. Was she occupied the entire time, or did she get easily bored? Did she ask you to play with her? How long did she spend on each activity during the session?

A week or more later, set aside another fifteen to twenty minutes to lead your child through some adult-directed musical play. Select several musical activities and guide her through each one, establishing the pace and the method of play. For instance, if you're playing together with a toy xylophone, attempt to instruct your child to play a certain tune or pattern. If you're singing together, choose the songs and invite your child to sing along with you. Once your music play has finished, jot down some notes about how engaged your child was with the play. Answer the same questions you answered in the first session, and also note whether you noticed any difference in her mood or behavior compared with the first session.

 ## THE HYPOTHESIS

Your child will be more engaged during the first session, in which she has more control over the choice of activities, than in the second session, which is adult led.

 ## THE RESEARCH

Researchers in a 2012 study looked at the factors that either promote or inhibit engagement during children's musical play. They observed parents and children who attended a series of music classes that involved weekly take-home assignments, such as conducting with flashlights. The class and home assignments presented opportunities for both open-ended activities in which children had relatively more control and adult-led activities in which children had relatively less control. Parents and researchers took notes throughout the series of classes, and the parents also participated in exit interviews at the end of the classes.

An analysis of the data found that a child's sense of agency influenced whether a particular activity encouraged or inhibited musical play. When children could choose between several options, or could invite an adult to play with them, it enhanced their play. But when activities were dictated by adults, and interaction mostly consisted of the adults prompting their children to follow instructions, the children seemed less engaged in play.

Other play-enhancing factors the study identified included opportunities for movement, availability of props, family interaction, and the opportunity to perform for a video recording. However, some of those same factors also sometimes led to inhibited play. If the child did not request to be recorded, for instance, the presence of a camera sometimes led him or her to stop playing.

For younger children, musical activities involving movement, instruments, and nonmusical vocalizations can be especially engaging. For instance, three-year-olds in a 2007 study tended not to sing along to songs, but they did engage by dancing, making motions, and using hand signs, and they also made non-singing vocalizations, such as the "woof woof" sounds in "How Much Is That Doggie in the Window?"

 **THE TAKEAWAY**

Keep in mind that it was not the presence of adults that inhibited children's musical play in the study described. Rather, it was children's perceived lack of agency. When the children were the ones directing the activities, inviting a parent to join in the fun made the play more fun, not less so. So be careful not to misinterpret these findings. Your child loves when you play with her. She just happens to feel more engaged when she gets to call the shots. There will be plenty of times when she will need to follow your lead and do what you say, but when it comes to playtime, let her take the reins.

Mobile Melodies

The family car is a place where kids are likely to engage in music-making activities, such as singing along to the radio or spontaneously singing or humming even when the car's sound system is off. A 2014 study looked at the ways preschoolers generate and experience music in the car. It found that children's music-making in transit was just as varied and enthusiastic as music-making in the home. Children who participated in the study routinely "sang, moved, listened to music, composed, and improvised" from their car seats.

The study also identified some qualities of the family car that make it ripe for musical exposure and expression. For one thing, it's relatively free of distractions. Children in the backseat typically don't have eye contact with the driver, and for some kids, that may make them feel more free to express themselves creatively without feeling embarrassed. And when the whole family drives somewhere together, it's a good opportunity for social music-making, such as sing-alongs and call-and-response songs.

If you're looking for more opportunities to spend quality time with your child and strengthen her love of music, a simple drive around town might be the answer.

13 Degrees of Distinction

AGE RANGE: 2 to 4 years

RESEARCH AREAS: Language development, communication

 THE EXPERIMENT

You'll need a sticker book that contains an assortment of stickers, preferably featuring some of the same characters in different poses or engaged in different actions, as well as six sheets of parchment paper and a digital camera, such as a cell phone camera.

Prior to the experiment, you will need to go through the sticker book and collect the stickers that will be used. There will be six trials, and in each trial your child will be asked to select from among either two or four stickers. For the three trials that will involve selecting from two stickers, choose characters that are dissimilar, such as a farmer and a dog. For each of these trials, place the two stickers onto a sheet of parchment paper and take a picture of one of the stickers. The remaining three trials will involve selecting from four stickers. In each of these trials, three of the characters should be similar and one should be dissimilar. For instance, you might select three stickers featuring a farmer in different poses and one sticker of a dog. For each trial, place the four stickers onto a sheet of parchment paper and take a picture of one of the three similar characters.

Have your child sit at a table. Explain that you are going to do a sticker hunt. You will show him a picture of a particular sticker on your camera or cell phone, then you will show him a sheet of parchment paper on which the sticker will appear along with other stickers. His job is to use words, not pointing, to identify the matching sticker. Once he correctly identifies the sticker, you can remove it from the parchment paper and give it to him as a prize.

Begin with a four-sticker trial, then alternate between two-sticker and four-sticker trials until you have done all six. If your child attempts to point to the sticker he wants, remind him that he has to use his words instead. During the two-sticker trials, a simple identifier, such as "the farmer" or "the dog," will suffice. But during the four-sticker trials, your child will need to use a more complex description to specify which of the three similar stickers he wants. If he uses an identifier that is not specific enough, such as "the farmer," you can prompt him to be more specific: "Which farmer? The farmer holding the bucket?" Allow him to continue until he has offered a description that applies to only one of the four stickers.

Note during each trial whether he begins with a simple or a complex description, and also take note of how many attempts he requires in each trial before correctly identifying the matching sticker.

THE HYPOTHESIS

Your child will learn to be as descriptive as necessary to unambiguously identify the matching character. In the four-sticker trials, he'll learn to give complex descriptions. But in the two-sticker trials, he will give only simple descriptions.

THE RESEARCH

Children in a 2012 study were shown two versions of a storybook, one of which had missing characters. They were then given the chance to select stickers representing the missing characters. In some trials, they could select from between two dissimilar stickers. For these trials, a simple identifier (e.g. "the farmer") sufficed. In other trials, there were four stickers to choose from, and three of the four were similar. In these trials, a more complex description (e.g. "The farmer with the hat") was required to unambiguously identify the matching sticker. The children were shown the arrays of either two or four stickers, and they had to use words, rather than pointing, to tell the experimenter which sticker they wanted.

With one group of children, if the child did not give enough information to unambiguously identify the desired sticker, the experimenter would give general feedback: "Which one do you need?" With another group of children, the experimenter would give specific feedback, such as "Do you need the daddy dancing or the daddy eating carrots?"

The researchers found that both two-year-olds and four-year-olds grew more likely, over the course of the trials, to offer complex descriptions for the four-sticker trials than for the two-sticker trials, suggesting that they recognized when complex descriptions were necessary or unnecessary, rather than merely learning to supply complex descriptions in all cases. Two main factors seemed to influence performance: age and feedback condition. The children who received specific feedback, rather than general feedback, were more likely to offer complex descriptions, presumably because they had the benefit of hearing the experimenters suggest some appropriate descriptions.

THE TAKEAWAY

Multiple complex skills are required to be able to complete the sticker identification task the way adults do. Your child needs to survey the options and detect the features that distinguish one from another. He must then determine the least complex description that unambiguously identifies a certain character from among multiple similar possibilities. Try teaching a computer to accomplish this task and you'll quickly realize that it's not as straightforward an exercise as you might think.

Specific feedback was shown to benefit performance, and that's something you can incorporate into your everyday interactions with your child. One way to give him opportunities to express himself while also supporting him when he struggles is a general-to-specific approach. For instance, suppose that at breakfast time he points to two cereal boxes on a shelf. You might start with a general question, such as "Which box do you want?" This allows him to name a particular cereal. But if he struggles to name one, you might try a more specific question: "Would you like the box with the tiger or the box with the rabbit?" This allows him to focus on the choice itself rather than on how to distinguish the options, but it also helps him learn one possible way to identify them. Through reinforcement, he'll gradually learn to do it himself.

14 Affirming Actions

AGE RANGE: 2 to 5 years

RESEARCH AREAS: Cognitive development, response bias

 THE EXPERIMENT

For this project, you will need a spoon, a spare toothbrush, and a soccer ball (or other ball of similar size). You are going to perform some actions using these objects and then quiz your child about what you have done.

First, use the spoon to make an eating motion. Then tell your child that you are going to ask her some questions about what you've just done, and that she can answer "yes," "no," or "I don't know" to each of them. Ask the following questions:

"Did I hold the spoon?"
"Did I bounce the spoon?"
"Did I twirno the spoon?"

Next, set the toothbrush on the ground and kick it, as if it were a ball. Then ask these questions:

"Did I kick the toothbrush?"
"Did I brush with the toothbrush?"
"Did I gloin the toothbrush?"

Finally, bounce the ball on the floor, then ask these questions:

"Did I bounce the ball?"
"Did I brush with the ball?"
"Did I plurm the ball?"

 ## THE HYPOTHESIS

If your child is a two-year-old, she is likely to answer "yes" to most of the questions, even those for which the appropriate answer is "no" or "I don't know." If your child is age three or older, she is likely to have answered "yes" and "no" appropriately, but to have answered "no" instead of "I don't know" for the questions with nonsense action words.

 ## THE RESEARCH

Children in a 2013 study were shown actions involving common objects, then asked a series of questions about what they saw.

They were directed to answer "yes," "no," or "I don't know" to the questions. During each trial, they were asked one question for which the correct answer was "yes," one for which the correct answer was "no," and one (involving a nonsense word) for which the correct answer was "I don't know."

Two-year-olds showed a strong "yes" bias. They tended to respond "yes" regardless of what the appropriate response would have been. By age three, however, that "yes" bias disappears. Children three and older tend to answer "yes" and "no" appropriately, but on the nonsense questions, in which "I don't know" is the appropriate answer, they tend to respond "no." (But it turns out that this is true even for adults. In the same study, adults were found to have roughly the same level of "no" bias for the nonsense questions as the children.)

These findings have surprisingly serious implications. For instance, if a doctor asks a young child about the nature of an injury, or an investigator is interviewing a child who witnessed a crime, being aware of these biases can be crucial to uncovering the truth or recognizing that the truth might be harder to uncover than it seems.

Even if your child is three or older and does not appear to exhibit a strong bias toward "yes" or "no," it may be worth repeating the experiment over time to confirm that a bias doesn't pop up unexpectedly.

THE TAKEAWAY

The results of this study suggest that when it's important to get accurate answers from your child, simple yes-or-no questions should probably be avoided, if possible. In cases in which alternate forms of questioning aren't working, try to structure your questions so that they are not leading and don't contain the expected answer. You might also want to try developmentally appropriate interviewing techniques, such as the Step-Wise technique, which involves beginning with general questions and drilling down to more specific questions only when required, or the Modified Structured Interview, which also goes from general to specific questions, and which uses questions that begin with who, what, when, where, and how to try to identify specific details. However, be aware that with any of these techniques, the deeper and more specific the questions get, the more likely it is that incorrect information may surface. Understanding children's biases will help you better know whether you can have confidence in the accuracy of their answers.

⑮ First Dibs

AGE RANGE: 2 to 5 years

RESEARCH AREAS: Social development, inferences

 THE EXPERIMENT

On three small pieces of paper, draw a boy, a girl, and a football.

On a flat surface, such as a table, place the drawings of the two children about a foot from each other. Then, place the football with one of the children. For the purpose of this description, it will be placed with the boy, but you can choose either of the children.

Explain to your child that you would like to tell him about the scene on the table. Use the following script, with directions in brackets:

"I have a story to tell you. Here we have a boy [*point to the boy*], and over here we have a girl [*point to the girl*]. Look what the boy is holding—it's a football! The boy plays with the football [*lift the football as if he's tossing it in the air and catching it*]. Then, the girl plays with the football [*move the football to the girl, and lift it as if she's tossing it in the air and catching it*]. Now that I've told you this story, I have a question: Whose football is it?"

Allow your child to respond. If he does not answer, or if he responds, "I don't know," tell the story over again and prompt him again to answer the question "Whose football is it?"

THE HYPOTHESIS

Your child will say that the first person who possessed the ball is the owner.

THE RESEARCH

Undergraduate students in a 2008 study were presented with a scenario much like the one you presented to your child. The students were asked which child owned the ball and which child liked the ball more. Although the students showed no bias with regard to which child liked the ball more, they did show a bias with regard to ownership. They chose the child who possessed the ball first at a rate much higher than chance. The author of the study suggests that one explanation for why first possessors are assumed to be owners is that there is a widely held legal doctrine pertaining to property rights that the first person who possesses a sought-after object gets to keep it. Maybe the legal doctrine influences our perception that first possessors are owners. Or maybe it's the other way around.

In a related 2008 study involving preschoolers, a similar scenario was presented involving a boy, a girl, and a ball. The results showed that just as with the college students, the preschoolers were more likely to identify the first child who played with the ball as its owner. Assuming these children were not familiar with the legal doctrine, these results suggest that there may be an innate bias toward viewing the first possessor as the owner.

 **THE TAKEAWAY**

Even young children tend to be aware of the "finders keepers" rule, and angry claims of "It's mine! I had it first!" have fueled many arguments between siblings and playmates. But it appears that these rudimentary rules of property rights may also operate at a deeper level, influencing our perception of who is the rightful owner, absent other, more pertinent information.

Now that you're aware of the potential for bias among both children and adults, it's an opportune time to discuss the ins and outs of ownership with your child:

- What does it mean to own something?

- How do I know that a toy belongs to someone else?

- If I'm not sure, how can I find out?

- If I own something, do I own it forever?

- If I don't own something, what do I need to do to be able to use it?

Work to Own

A 2010 study found that preschoolers were more likely than adults to indicate that a person who creatively transforms an item acquires ownership of that item. In the study, participants were told that one set of clay was theirs and another set was the experimenter's. Then, the experimenter traded with them and reshaped the clay to form a new design. Participants were then asked whose clay it was. A large majority of the preschoolers said it was now the experimenter's clay, while only about a quarter of adults indicated that the ownership had transferred. So, while young children might ordinarily ascribe ownership based on who possesses an item first, this study makes clear that there are exceptions, and that when creative labor is invested, it can affect how children perceive ownership of property.

The Effect of Causes

AGE RANGE: 3 to 4 years

RESEARCH AREA: Language development

 THE EXPERIMENT

You are going to help your child learn the names of the three imaginary creatures shown on the next page. Above each picture is the creature's name, and below each is a description of the creature. Begin by pointing to each creature, in whatever order you like, and reading the description without reading the creature's name. Then, in the same order as before, point to each creature and identify it, repeating its name several times. For instance, for the first image you might say, "This is a Treedew. It's a really cool Treedew. Remember, a Treedew uses its long arms to reach things way up high."

Now take about three to five minutes to play with your child,

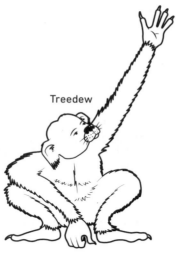

Treedew

A Treedew uses its long arms to
reach things way up high.

Branist

Wilmop

A Branist has hard scales,
a long tail, and a good sense of smell.

A Wilmop is an imaginary creature
not many people know about.

then return to the images and quiz her. First, ask your child to find the Branist, and note whether she points to the second image. Next, ask your child to find the Wilmop, and note whether she points to the third image. Finally, ask your child to find the Treedew, and note whether she points to the first image.

About a week later, return to the pictures. Without any review session, quiz your child again in the same manner as before. Then, for each creature, ask your child if she remembers anything special about it, and note whether her description matches the one that accompanies the image.

 ## THE HYPOTHESIS

During the first quiz, the odds of your child correctly identifying each creature is about 50 percent each time. But during the second quiz, a week after you introduced the characters, your child will likely be able to correctly identify the Treedew, although her ability to correctly identify the others will still not be higher than 50 percent.

 ## THE RESEARCH

A 2009 study looked at whether preschoolers might be more likely to learn novel labels for unfamiliar creatures if the creatures were described in terms of their causal properties—that is, what kinds of things they do—as opposed to noncausal properties, such as what they look like. The preschoolers were shown a book containing Pokémon characters. For one set of characters, they were given a causal description of something the character could do. For another set, they were given a noncausal description that didn't allude to anything the character could do. And for a third set, which acted as a baseline, they were given a vague description that did not convey anything specific about the character. The children were then taught the names of the characters, and they were tested a short time later about what they had learned. In the first test, they were told the name of a character and asked to point to its picture. In the second test, they were shown a character and asked to recall its name. These tests were repeated about a week later.

The study's author found that during the first set of tests, the children's ability to correctly identify each character didn't differ from chance, regardless of which condition they were in. But when the children were tested again a week later, those in the baseline and noncausal conditions performed about the same, while those in the causal condition did significantly better than chance.

In the experiment you performed with your child, the Treedew had a causal description that referred to its ability to reach up high. The Branist had a noncausal description referring to its appearance. And the Wilmop's description was a control; it did not describe the creature's abilities or appearance. Out of the three creatures, your child was most likely to remember the name of the creature with a causal description: the Treedew.

One possible explanation for why causal information appears to help children learn and remember novel words better than other types of information is that both children and adults tend to have a particularly strong capacity for remembering relationships between things, and since every cause has an effect, there is a sort of built-in relationship between the two that might aid in word acquisition.

What explains the fact that the children's performance in the causal condition got better over time? The study points out that sleep appears to help children process newly learned information, and the more complex or abstract the information, the more helpful that processing is. Cause-and-effect relationships are both complex and abstract, so it stands to reason that when children in the causal condition were given an opportunity to "sleep on it," they would have had better luck identifying the new labels they had learned.

 **THE TAKEAWAY**

Your child has a knack for picking up new words, and sometimes it seems as if it all happens so effortlessly that she hardly needs help with the task. But the results of this study suggest that you actually can make language acquisition easier for her, at least to a degree. Presenting descriptions that tell your child what sorts of things an animate or inanimate object can do gives those words a sort of mental stickiness that help her better identify the object later. So when you're introducing new things to your child, think of ways that you can describe them in terms of their function. And when you're introducing animals or people, try to touch on the interesting abilities they have and what they like to do.

🔟7 Symbols Crash

AGE RANGE: 3 to 4 years

RESEARCH AREAS: Language development, communication

 THE EXPERIMENT

Photocopy and cut out the six pictograms that accompany this project on page 245. Three of the pictograms represent people: a man, a woman, and a baby. The other three represent actions: push, pull, and hold.

Explain to your child that these symbols represent words that can help you tell a story. Show him each of the six pictograms and say what word they represent. Now show him how the pictograms can be arranged to form a sentence. Place the "woman," "hold," and "baby" pictograms in sequence and explain that these symbols represent the sentence "The woman holds the baby."

Now show your child Scene 1 (page 245). Explain that in the scene a woman is pushing a baby in a stroller, and ask your child to select and arrange pictograms that describe what is happening. Note whether your child selects the correct pictograms that represent the subject ("woman"), verb ("push"), and object ("baby"), and whether he places them in the correct order.

Now explain that you're going to arrange some pictograms to form a sentence. Place the "woman," "push," and "man" pictograms next to one another, and show your child the sentence you've constructed, but don't describe it. Then ask him to look at the three scenes on page 246 and select which scene is represented by the pictograms. Note whether the scene he chooses contains the subject, verb, and object, and whether they're in the same order as in the pictograms.

 THE HYPOTHESIS

Your child is likely to understand that the pictograms represent people or actions and that the pictograms can be arranged to form complete thoughts. Nevertheless, he is unlikely to successfully complete the first challenge. And for the second challenge, he is just as likely to choose an incorrect answer as he is to choose the correct answer.

Most children develop verbal communication abilities within their first few years, but a variety of conditions can delay or inhibit speech. Children who are nonverbal often use alternative communication methods, such as tablets or other devices that allow them to communicate. Older children can sometimes type or point to letters to form language, but for young children who are unable to read or write, these assistive communication devices typically display a catalog of symbols. When the child touches a symbol, the corresponding word is displayed or spoken by the device.

Researchers in a 2010 study wanted to explore whether constructing and interpreting sentences using pictograms might be difficult even for children without disabilities. They had three- and four-year-old children complete two tasks similar to those your child completed. In the first task, called the transposition task, each participant was shown a scene in which there was a primary action that could be represented with a subject-verb-object structure. The experimenter gave a spoken representation of that primary action, such as "The clown is pushing the boy." Then, the child was asked to place pictograms on a board to communicate the same message using symbols. In the second task, called the interpretation task, the child was shown a sequence of pictograms and was asked to identify which scene from a group of pictures was accurately described by the symbols.

The researchers found that in the transposition task, most of the children selected the correct noun symbols, but many neglected the verb or arranged the pictograms in an order other than subject-verb-object, which is the order the children were most familiar with in their spoken language. In addition, across multiple trials, relatively few children maintained a consistent ordering of the pictograms. In the interpretation task, the pre-schoolers fared slightly better. On average, the participants identified the correct scene from among several possibilities in 51 percent of trials, but only about half of them showed consistency across trials, and among those children, almost a third consistently treated the object of the sentence as the subject. Furthermore, good performance on one of the two tasks was not associated with good performance on the other.

All of these findings suggest that using pictograms to construct complete thoughts is a difficult task for typically developing three- and four-year-old children. Even though their language skills are strong and they can easily string together complete sentences in spoken language, those skills do not easily translate to using graphic symbols.

This has implications for parents, caregivers, teachers, and clinicians who work with children who require alternative communication devices. For instance, parents and caregivers might need to be flexible in their interpretation of a sequence of pictograms because the ordering may be different from what would likely be expected in a spoken utterance. And because verbs were often omitted during the experimental trials, teachers and clinicians might need to spend extra time helping children to use verbs, which are necessary for more complex communication.

Earlier research led by one of the same authors found that between the ages of four and seven, children do make marked improvements in their ability to interpret pictographic representations of sentences, so it may be worthwhile to repeat this project as your child gets older to see if his responses change.

🔍 THE TAKEAWAY

Even if your child has no language delays and does not require an assistive communication device, there are some practical things you can take away from this experiment. First, keep in mind that your child's proficiency with spoken language does not necessarily mean that he is developmentally ready to read or write. Even a child who can recognize a few sight words may not yet be able to string them together to form a grammatical sentence. Second, remember that for most young children, spoken language is their only language. Whereas older children and adults have typically mastered the language of interior thought and of the written word, preschoolers may struggle to express themselves, or to even process their own thoughts, without the use of spoken language. So if your child is a chatterbox, as many are, please be patient and recognize that at this age, it's completely developmentally appropriate.

18 Less Is More

AGE RANGE: 3 to 4 years

RESEARCH AREAS: Cognitive development, executive function, impulsiveness

 THE EXPERIMENT

Gather up small treats that can be used as rewards, such as jelly beans, raisins, or chocolate chips—whichever will be the most enticing to your child. Place two treats on one small plate and five treats on another. Explain to your child that you're going to play a game in which she can earn treats. The trick to the game is that whichever plate she points to, she'll earn the treats on the *other* plate. Play at least six rounds of the game, switching up which plate contains two and which plate contains five treats. Note how frequently your child points to the plate

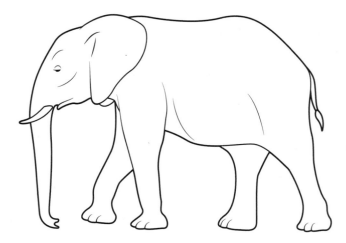

with fewer treats, and how often she points to the plate with more treats.

Sometime later, explain that you are going to play a similar game, except you will use the two illustrations that accompany this project. The mouse illustration will represent the plate of two treats, and the elephant illustration will represent the plate of five treats. Remind your child that whichever illustration she points to, she'll earn the treats represented by the *other* picture. So if she points to the mouse illustration, she'll earn five treats, and if she points to the elephant illustration, she'll earn two treats. Again, play several rounds of the game, switching up which illustration you hold in each hand, and note how frequently your child points to the mouse and how frequently she points to the elephant.

THE HYPOTHESIS

If your child is three years old, and particularly if she is not yet three and a half, she is likely to either consistently choose the plate with more treats or consistently choose the plate with fewer treats. If she is four years old, she is likely to choose the plate with fewer treats more frequently, and if she starts out by choosing the plate with more treats, she is likely to improve over the course of the trials.

THE RESEARCH

In two related experiments, researchers in a 2005 study led preschoolers in a task that was originally developed to test chimpanzees' ability to inhibit an impulsive response. In the first experiment, the children were presented with groups of two and five candies, and they were told that if they pointed to one of the groups, they would receive the candies from the other group.

Three-year-olds, particularly those on the younger side, tended to either do consistently well (earning five treats instead of two in each trial) or consistently poorly (earning two treats instead of five). Those who started out poorly did not appear to improve their performance over the course of multiple trials, suggesting that they were unable to stop themselves from pointing toward the group of candies they wanted, even though they appeared to understand the rules of the game.

Four-year-olds, on the other hand, tended to perform better on the task overall, and even those who started out poorly tended to show improvement as the trials continued.

In the second experiment, the researchers repeated the task, but this time, they used symbolic representations of the rewards. A picture of a mouse represented the group of two candies, and a picture of an elephant represented the group of five candies. The researchers found that the children did better on the task than in the first experiment, in which the participants had to point to the candies themselves. In fact, three-year-olds' performance in the second experiment was very close to four-year-olds' performance in the first experiment.

These results were similar to those in the earlier study involving chimps, in which the primates fairly consistently pointed to the larger group of candies (thus earning the smaller reward). But when they were asked to point to either a numeral 2 or a numeral 5, each of the chimp participants caught on quickly and pointed to the numeral 2 (thus earning the larger reward) more than twice as often as they had when pointing to the real candies.

The authors of the 2005 study concluded that in preschool-aged children, as with the chimpanzees, a more abstract, symbolic representation of a reward can help inhibit impulsive behavior.

 **THE TAKEAWAY**

Chances are, a good deal of your child's mischievous behavior boils down to impulsivity. You might rehearse, "Please don't touch anything" on the way to the store, and your child might repeat back, "Don't touch anything," when asked what the expectation is, yet nevertheless she'll reach for the candy displayed at her eye level during checkout. It's almost as if the "Don't touch anything" instruction she's trying to remember gets clobbered by the much more intense *"I WANT THAT NOW"* impulse.

It's not possible to replace all real-world temptations with more symbolic stimuli, but your child is likely at a point where she has acquired enough language skills that she can use words, rather than point to physical objects, to make decisions or express preferences. And words are themselves a symbolic representation of the things to which they refer. You can also set the stage for reflective, rather than impulsive, decision making by allowing your child to make decisions in a calm, unhurried environment. For instance, next time you visit a buffet-style restaurant for a family meal, you might want to discuss and decide on healthy food choices on the ride to the restaurant, rather than waiting until you're in the buffet line, staring at the alluring french fries and the not-as-alluring broccoli.

⑲ Majority Rulers

AGE RANGE: 3 to 4 years

RESEARCH AREAS: Social development, deference

THE EXPERIMENT

You'll need three strips of rigid material, such as wooden dowels, foam board, or thick strips of cardboard. One strip should be 12 inches long, another 11, and the third 10. You'll also need two blocks or small boxes of equal height, as well as a small doll or action figure and some stickers to use as rewards.

Recruit three friends or family members to act as participants. Show your child the three strips, then ask each of the three friends which is the big strip. The first friend should point to one of the two smaller strips, and the other two friends should indicate the same strip as the first friend. Then, ask your child to point to the big strip, and note whether he points to the strip that is actually the biggest or whether he agrees with the consensus. Take a break and rearrange the strips, then repeat the procedure.

Now place the two blocks 11.5 inches apart, wide enough that the longest strip can rest on them but the other two strips cannot. Place the doll next to one block and the sticker next to the other. Explain to your child that the doll is on one side of a river, and the sticker is on the other side. To help the doll get the sticker, one of the three strips can be placed across the two blocks to form a bridge. But only the biggest of the three strips is long enough to form the bridge.

Again, have the three friends indicate which is the biggest strip. The friends should again all agree that one of the smaller strips is the biggest. Then, ask your child to select the big strip and place it across the blocks to form a bridge. Note which strip he selects.

 ## THE HYPOTHESIS

The first time your helpers offer an incorrect consensus, your child is likely to ignore their influence and correctly identify the biggest strip. But if he does defer to their opinion, he is less likely to do so the second time they offer an incorrect consensus. And the third time, during the bridge-building part of the experiment, it is highly unlikely that he will defer to their consensus, even if he did the previous two times.

THE RESEARCH

Three- and four-year-old children in a 2010 study were shown three strips of foam board, each of a different size. Three adult actors looked at the strips, and when asked to identify the biggest strip, all three pointed to one of the smaller strips. The children were then asked which of the three strips was the biggest. This was repeated for a total of four trials.

The researchers found that about 60 percent of three-year-olds and 75 percent of four-year-olds correctly identified the longest strip in all four trials. Of the children who did not correctly identify the longest strip in a trial, they invariably selected the strip that had been chosen by the adults. However, as the trials progressed, the children became less likely to defer to the consensus.

A follow-up experiment looked at whether children would defer to the consensus at the same rate if a practical goal were introduced. Each child was told that a toy rabbit needed to build a bridge to cross a river and obtain a sticker to share with the child, and only the biggest of the three foam strips was long enough to fit on two bridge ends. Again, adult actors agreed that one of the smaller strips was the biggest, and then the children were asked to point to the biggest strip. After giving their answer, they were invited to place the biggest strip on the bridge ends to see if it fit.

As in the first experiment, the researchers found that a

minority of the children deferred to the incorrect consensus when asked to point to the biggest strip. Yet when it came time to place the biggest strip on the bridge ends, every child, regardless of whether he or she had deferred to the consensus, selected the strip that was *actually* the longest and was able to construct the bridge and earn the prize.

 ## THE TAKEAWAY

There appear to be several reasons why some preschoolers defer to the majority even when they know the majority is wrong. Some of it has to do with cultural expectations, some with age, and some with the child's general level of assuredness. But across the four trials in this study, even children who were initially willing to defer to adult consensus grew more resistant, suggesting that it doesn't take much for your child to begin asserting himself. Indeed, the results of this study suggest that a desirable goal, such as a sticker, is enough to make children abandon any social graces that might otherwise lead them to fall in with the crowd. What you, as a parent, can take away from this research probably depends on your own expectations for your child. Although in this contrived experiment the adults are clearly in the wrong, there may be other times when your child is less certain about whether persons in authority are correct. You might be the type of parent who insists that in this sort of situation, your child must trust his instincts and assume the authority figures have got it wrong, or you might be the type of parent who thinks your child should be open to the possibility that his elders know more than he thinks they do. Spend some time talking through a few possible scenarios with your child to help him better understand your point of view. For instance, suppose a teacher tells him to fetch some crayons from one cabinet in the classroom, but he knows that the crayons are actually kept in a different cabinet. What should he do? Is it more likely that the teacher is mistaken about the crayons' location, or that she has moved the crayons to the new location and is not mistaken about where they now reside? Having discussions about these possibilities can help your child feel more confident about what to do when he encounters such a situation in real life.

Abandoning the Pack

In a 2015 study, children watched a group of people demonstrate how to open a puzzle box. Then, a lone individual demonstrated how to open it using a different approach. When both the group and the individual were successful in opening the box, the children preferred to copy the method demonstrated by the group. But when only the individual was successful, the children reversed course and preferred to copy the approach demonstrated by the individual.

The study's authors concluded that while kids have a natural tendency to follow the crowd, they also tend to copy people who are successful at reaching desirable goals, and when these two tendencies are in competition, proficiency can win out over popularity.

⓴ What Speaks Louder?

AGE RANGE: 3 to 5 years

RESEARCH AREAS: Social/emotional development, language development

 THE EXPERIMENT

There are two phases to this project, the second of which is optional. For the first phase, you'll need sweetened and unsweetened Kool-Aid, or other powdered drink packets, sufficient to make four cups. If possible, select different flavors and colors so it's obvious that each cup is different from the others. For the second phase, you'll need an additional four cups.

Enlist a friend's help and give her some instructions ahead of time. She will taste each of the drinks as your child watches, and she should react to either the pleasant sweet or unpleasant sour taste using both facial expressions and words. Her facial expressions should always match her genuine reaction, but in some cases her words should not.

For the first sweet drink, tell her to react naturally, with a pleased facial expression and words such as "This tastes good!" For the first sour drink, she should again react naturally, with a frown and words such as "This isn't good."

But for the next two drinks, she should use words that don't match her facial expression. For the sweet drink, she should react with a pleased facial expression but with the words "This isn't good." And for the next sour drink, she should react with a frown but with the words "This tastes good."

Now that you've enlisted your helper, it's time to do the experiment. Have your friend sit on one end of a table with the four prepared cups of Kool-Aid in clear glasses, and position your child at the other end of the table. Tell your child that your friend is going to taste each of the four drinks, and your child gets to guess whether the friend likes or dislikes each one.

After each taste, prompt your child to make a guess.

In the optional second phase of the experiment, you'll repeat the same scenario using a different friend as a helper. But this time, instead of natural expressions, the friend should exaggerate her nonverbal reactions. For the sweet drinks, that exaggerated reaction might include licking her lips and rubbing her belly contentedly. For the sour drinks, it might include shuddering and wiping the taste off her mouth.

THE HYPOTHESIS

Your child will make accurate guesses when the facial expressions and words are consistent with one another. When the facial expressions and words are inconsistent, your child will probably rely on the verbal cue in the first phase but on the nonverbal cue in the second phase.

THE RESEARCH

In a 2003 study involving children between ages three and five, the participants watched short video clips in which an actor drank from a cup and responded with facial expressions that matched her actual reaction, but sometimes with words that were inconsistent with her reaction. In some of the video clips, the actor's reaction was natural and in others it was exaggerated.

The researchers found that nearly all of the children were able to accurately gauge whether the actor liked or disliked the drink when her actions and words were consistent with one another. But when the actions and words were inconsistent, the children relied more heavily on the verbal cues when the response was natural, but more heavily on the nonverbal cues when the reaction was exaggerated.

The results of this study indicate that in at least some cases, children as young as three years will rely more on nonverbal cues than on verbal cues when trying to resolve an inconsistent response. This was unexpected, because prior research had found that this behavior doesn't show up until age nine or ten. Prior to that age, children have a "lexical bias" when it comes to interpreting these inconsistent reactions, even though in many real-world cases, it's the actions that speak louder than words, rather than the other way around. The researchers think the exaggerated nature of the reaction may have been the critical factor that brought out the response in preschool-aged children.

The researchers point to several developmental skills that influence whether children lean toward verbal or nonverbal cues. Another study, for instance, showed that babies tend to use mostly emotional cues to resolve inconsistencies, but as they show progress with language acquisition, that shifts, and they begin to rely more on verbal cues. Preschoolers are also beginning to pick up on social rules that lead people to say things they don't really mean, such as feigning happiness about an unwanted gift in an effort to be polite, so those social rules may lead them to discount the words and pay more attention to the nonverbal response.

 **THE TAKEAWAY**

Young children are notoriously bad at understanding sarcasm and other situations in which you don't really mean the words you say. They're also just starting to pick up on complex social rules that provide meaningful context for speech, and they may struggle to apply that context appropriately. So give your child a break and follow this simple maxim: Say what you mean, and mean what you say. It will lead to less confusion, and it will also model honest, direct communication.

㉑ Focusing Exercise

AGE RANGE: 3 to 5 years

RESEARCH AREAS: Memory and attention, physical activity

 THE EXPERIMENT

For this project, you'll need an age-appropriate seek-and-find book, where target images are hidden within a busy scene. After a period of relatively sedentary activity, during which your child remains fairly still (such as being read a story), spend five to ten minutes guiding her through the seek-and-find book, taking note of how often she correctly identifies the target images and incorrectly identifies other images as the targets. Sometime later, engage your child in twenty to thirty minutes of moderate to vigorous physical activity (such as playing hopscotch or tag). Then spend another five to ten minutes guiding her through more pages of the seek-and-find book, again keeping track of how often she correctly and incorrectly identifies the targets.

 ## THE HYPOTHESIS

Your child will demonstrate longer sustained attention, measured by the accuracy and completeness of her target identification, after the period of physical activity, compared with her performance after the period of sedentary activity.

 ## THE RESEARCH

A 2008 study had shown that physical exercise improved adolescents' performance on a test of attention and concentration. Researchers in a 2012 study wanted to see whether physical activity might have the same effect on preschool-age children. Each child completed a seek-and-find test after a period of sedentary activity and again after a period of physical activity. The researchers found that the children overlooked significantly fewer target images after the physical activity than after the sedentary activity, suggesting that they were better able to sustain focus during the task.

One possible explanation the researchers offered for the experiment's results is that complex motor skills, such as throwing or catching a ball or avoiding obstacles while running, require sustained mental focus. Thus, when children engage in physical exercise, their brains become primed to sustain attention, and that effect can carry over when they move on to a purely cognitive activity, like the seek-and-find.

THE TAKEAWAY

It's no surprise that young children enjoy active play. Most boys and girls in this age group need little adult encouragement to run, skip, dance, tumble, or jump. What may be surprising, however, is that physical activity can strengthen a child's ability to focus on mental tasks that follow. This has implications for how parents and teachers might put together a child's daily routine. Although recess and outside play are often treated as cool-down periods following structured activities or instructional time, it may actually be to your child's advantage to make physical exercise a warm-up period that prepares her for an activity that requires sustained focus.

22 Paw Presence

AGE RANGE: 3 to 5 years

RESEARCH AREAS: Memory and attention, animal interaction

 THE EXPERIMENT

For this experiment, you will need to enlist the help of a dog who is friendly with children—either your own or a pet who is part of a friend's or a relative's family. You will also need to photocopy and cut out the twelve picture cards on page 247. Half of the pictures have a farm theme and half have an ocean theme. For both themes, some of the pictures depict animate objects and some depict inanimate objects. Finally, you will need two envelopes.

For the first part of the experiment, select three pictures of animate objects and three pictures of inanimate objects. Sit with your child and explain that you have pictures from two places—a farm and an ocean—and you would like to sort them so that all the farm pictures go in one envelope and all the ocean pictures go in the other envelope. One by one, show your child a picture card, say the name of the person, animal, or object pictured, and ask him to place it into either the farm envelope or the ocean envelope. Make a note of how accurately he is able to sort the pictures.

For the second part of the experiment, which you can do a short time later or on another day, you will repeat the process with the remaining six picture cards, only this time, explain that the dog would like to look at each picture before it goes into its envelope. Each time you produce a picture card, show it not only to your child but also to the dog. Then say the name of the person, animal, or object pictured, and direct your child to sort the picture card into one of the two envelopes, as before.

 THE HYPOTHESIS

In the first part of the experiment, your child will sort the pictures of animate and inanimate objects with roughly the same amount of accuracy. But in the second part of the experiment, when the dog is present, he will sort the picture cards depicting animate objects more accurately than those depicting inanimate objects.

In a 2012 study, children were divided into three groups and asked to sort farm and ocean pictures into their proper photo albums. In one group, an adult researcher was present in the room. In another group, the researcher was joined by a miniature poodle who had visited the children's classroom a few times before. In a third group, the researcher was joined by a stuffed toy dog. In both the real-dog and toy-dog groups, the pictures were shown to the dog, who was ostensibly observing the sorting task.

The researchers found that the children in the no-dog and stuffed-dog groups classified animate and inanimate pictures with roughly the same degree of accuracy. Children in the real-dog group classified inanimate pictures with similar accuracy to the other groups, but they were better at classifying animate objects. The study suggests that the presence of a dog, which itself is animate, helps children better recognize other animate objects.

These results support a growing body of evidence that the presence of an animal can help children maintain focus on a number of different tasks. For instance, in a 2010 study with the same lead author, preschoolers were found to need fewer instructional prompts to complete a cognitive task when a dog was present during the task.

 **THE TAKEAWAY**

It's true that pets can sometimes distract us from our work. But the results of this study suggest that a well-trained, friendly dog can actually help young children improve their focus on the task at hand. If you have pets at home, or if you have visits with friends or family members who have pets, feel free to allow them to join your child for story time and other skill-building and educational activities. Not only is it fun to snuggle up with a furry friend, but it also might boost your child's brain power.

23 On Premises

AGE RANGE: 3 to 5 years

RESEARCH AREAS: Social development, reasoning, peer interactions

THE EXPERIMENT

For this project, you will present two similar activities to your child and a same-age friend, such as a classmate or neighbor.

For the first activity, you will need four cardboard boxes or other containers. Place a rubber band and a rock in the first box. In the second, place

a juice box and a bottle of ketchup. In the third, place some squares of toilet paper and a book. Leave the final box empty.

Gather your child and her friend together and explain that you are going to introduce them to the creature pictured on page 105. Tell the children that the creature is called a mibb, and there are three unusual things about it. The first unusual thing is that it only eats rubber bands—nothing else. The second unusual thing is that it only drinks ketchup—nothing else. And the third unusual thing is that it only sleeps on toilet paper—nothing else.

Present the three boxes with items inside and explain that the mibb is going on a trip and needs to pack one item from each box in its suitcase (represented by the empty box). Ask the children to work together to help the mibb choose a useful item from each box and place it in the suitcase. Then, allow them to work without your help, but be sure to listen carefully to how they talk to each other as they complete the task.

Sometime later, you can present the second activity. This time, you'll need an adult helper to assist you. Again, you'll need four cardboard boxes or other containers. Place a tennis ball and a small toy in the first box. In the second, place a white sock and a piece of paper. In the third, place a pencil case and a spoon. Leave the fourth box empty.

Have the adult helper take your child's friend out of the room to play while you introduce your child to the creature pictured on page 106. Tell your child that the creature is called a kreet, and there are three unusual things about it. The first unusual thing is that it only eats tennis balls—nothing else. The second unusual thing is that it only wears white socks—nothing else. And the third unusual thing is that it only sleeps in pencil cases—nowhere else.

Now bring the other child back into the room and present the three boxes with items inside. Explain that the kreet is going on a trip and needs to pack one item from each box in its suitcase (represented by the empty box). Ask the children to work together to help the kreet choose a useful item from each box and place it in the suitcase. Then, allow them to work together without your help. Again, listen carefully to how they talk to each other as they complete the task.

❓ THE HYPOTHESIS

The children will mention the three unusual properties of the creature, such as "They eat tennis balls" or "This is what they sleep in," more frequently during the second activity than during the first.

📖 THE RESEARCH

Researchers in a 2016 study were curious about whether preschoolers understand enough about what other children know or do not know that they adapt their arguments according to whether they have shared knowledge about a premise.

When psychologists look at how people make joint decisions, they sometimes break down each person's argument into its main components. One component is a proposal, such as "We should place this item in the kreet's suitcase." A second component is evidence, such as "It is a tennis ball." And a third component is a premise, also called a warrant, which shows why the presented evidence justifies the proposal, such as "Kreets eat tennis balls."

When adults make joint decisions, that last component—the premise—is often implied but goes unstated, particularly when they understand that everyone else involved in the decision-making process shares the same knowledge about that premise.

But when one decision maker knows, or has reason to believe, that another person involved in the decision doesn't know about the premise, that decision maker is more likely to mention the premise explicitly, in order to spell it out for the other person.

In the 2016 study, pairs of children were divided into three groups. In one group, called the common-ground group, both children in the pair learned about the unusual qualities of an imaginary creature and then had to perform a sorting task similar to the one in this project. In another group, called the one-expert group, only one of the children learned about the imaginary creature's unusual qualities before the pair completed the sorting task. And in a third group, called the two-expert group, both children in the pair learned about the imaginary creature's qualities, but not at the same time.

The researchers found that the children in the common-ground group were less likely than children in the other two groups to explicitly mention the premise, presumably because it was understood that their partner already knew about and understood the premise, since their partner had been present when it was explained to them. That did not hold true, however, for the two-expert group. Both children had knowledge of the premises, but the justifications they offered for their arguments were more similar to those offered in the one-expert group than those offered in the common-ground group. This result suggests that young children have difficulty recognizing whether they and their partner have shared knowledge if it was not acquired as part of a shared experience.

Being able to persuade a partner when making joint decisions can be a difficult task even for an adult. It draws on your capacity to reason and to understand complex social dynamics. For instance, your partner's personality and his or her existing view of the world must be taken into account. If it's a complex task for an adult, imagine how much more complex it is for a child. By preschool, children have acquired some capacity to understand that there are often differences between what they know and what other people know, but there's still progress to be made on that front. They're also still learning about how to work well with others, how to "read" a person's unspoken communication, how to deal with different personality types, and how to reason about the world. The good news is that most preschoolers are eager to improve these skills, so giving them impromptu lessons in the course of everyday affairs—such as "Your friend already knows that mibbs only eat rubber bands, because she also learned all about mibbs"—can help them correct the course when necessary.

Moral Appeals

When preschoolers recognize that they and others share knowledge about a premise, it affects the sort of justifications they make for their arguments. That common ground also comes into play when they make judgments about rules of morality. For instance, children in a 2018 study were paired up and asked to jointly decide whether to reward or punish a storybook character who had violated either a social rule (such as placing a yellow toy in a box designated for green toys only) or a moral rule (such as stealing a classmate's belongings).

The researchers found that the children were more likely to explicitly state the premises for social rules than for moral rules. What might explain the difference? The researchers argue that children are less likely to assume a shared knowledge of social rules because they conceive of those rules as relatively arbitrary and limited in application. In contrast, they are more likely to assume a shared knowledge of basic moral rules, such as the wrongness of stealing, because they conceive of those rules as fundamental, universal, and self-evident.

㉔ Dubious Advice

AGE RANGE: 3 to 5 years

RESEARCH AREAS: Social development, trust

 THE EXPERIMENT

You'll need two small opaque containers and an assortment of small stickers to use as prizes. You'll also need to recruit one adult friend to play a helper role and another adult friend to play a trickster role.

Tell your child that you are going to play a game in which he will guess which of two containers has a sticker under it. If he guesses correctly, he gets the sticker as a prize. Introduce the friend who will play the role of the helper, and explain that the friend will be the one who places the sticker under one of the containers. Say that you are going to play two rounds of the game yourself, to demonstrate how it works, and then your child will get a chance to play.

For both of the demonstration rounds, turn your back while the helper places a sticker under one of the two containers. When you turn around, the helper should point to the container under which the sticker is hidden and say, "You should pick this one." Follow the helper's advice, and when you lift the container to reveal the sticker, the helper should smile and say, "Yes!" to indicate that she is pleased with the outcome.

Then, give your child a chance to play the game. Direct him to turn his back while the helper places a sticker under one of the containers. When your child turns around, the helper should point to the container under which the sticker is hidden and say, "You should pick this one." Allow your child to select a container, and note whether he follows or ignores the helper's advice.

Sometime later, you will play this game again, only this time, it will be with the friend who is going to play the role of the trickster. Tell your child that you are going to play the same game as before, and introduce your second friend, who will hide the sticker under one of the containers. As before, you are going to do two demonstration rounds, then let your child play.

For both of the demonstration rounds, turn your back while the trickster places a sticker under one of the two containers. When you turn around, the trickster should point to the container that does not have a sticker hidden under it and say, "You should pick this one." Follow the helper's advice, and when you lift the container and discover there is no sticker, the trickster should smile and say, "Yes!" to indicate that he is pleased with the outcome.

Now allow your child to play. Direct him to turn his back while the friend places a sticker under one of the containers. When your child turns around, the trickster should again point to the container with no sticker under it and say, "You should pick this one." Allow your child to select a container, and note whether he follows or ignores the helper's advice.

 ## THE HYPOTHESIS

Your child, regardless of age, is likely to follow the helper's advice. But when it's the trickster's turn to give advice, your child's response depends on his age. Children under age five are likely to follow the trickster's advice, but five-year-olds are equally likely to trust or to ignore the trickster's advice.

 ## THE RESEARCH

Preschoolers in a 2001 study were divided into two groups. Both groups watched video clips of a person playing the sticker-finding game, assisted by a pointer. In the clips seen by the first group of children, the pointer would point to one of the two containers and say, "You should pick that one." When the game player selected the suggested container, they discovered the sticker, and the pointer smiled and said, "Yes!" to indicate that she was pleased with the outcome. In the clips seen by the second group, the pointer also pointed to one of the two containers and said, "You should pick that one." But when the game player followed the pointer's suggestion, they discovered that there was no sticker under it. Nevertheless, the pointer smiled and said, "Yes!" to indicate that she was pleased with the outcome.

Then, the children were allowed to play the game themselves, assisted by the pointer they had seen in the video clips. The pointer then pointed to one of the containers and said, "You should pick this one."

The researchers found that more than 90 percent of the three-year-olds followed the pointer's advice, regardless of whether they had watched the video clips of the pointer being a helper or a trickster. Among four-year-olds, about 69 percent followed the helper's advice, while 60 percent followed the trickster's advice. But with five-year-olds, the spread between trust of helpers and trust of tricksters was more pronounced. About 71 percent followed the helper's advice, while only about half followed the trickster's advice.

Somewhat paradoxically, in follow-up questions about the video clips they had seen, the four-year-olds were generally able to identify whether the pointer was trying to help or trick the game player. Yet they nevertheless followed the pointer's advice more often than not.

The researchers argue that children at this age might be able to recognize deceptive behavior, but may struggle to use that information to make future predictions about intent. Or it could be the case that they are able to factor in that information, yet their generally trusting nature overrides any red flags that the previous deceptive episodes might raise.

✦ THE TAKEAWAY

Regardless of the exact mechanism that explains the children's performance in this experiment, the practical conclusion is clear. Preschoolers, by and large, tend to be trusting and compliant rather than skeptical when an adult gives them advice or instruction, even in situations in which the person has clearly demonstrated untrustworthy conduct. In this project, the deception is innocuous, but it doesn't take much creativity to imagine scenarios that could have far more dire consequences. Thus, it's important for parents to both protect and educate their children about deception. Parents can protect their children by only entrusting them to the care of qualified, trustworthy caregivers. And they can educate their children by talking to them in age-appropriate terms about how to identify safe adults they can turn to when they need help, what constitutes good touch versus bad touch, respecting personal boundaries, and how to distinguish between good and bad secrets. One way to explain the latter is that good secrets are always temporary and conceal something in order to make someone happy, as when we keep a surprise party a secret until the guest of honor arrives. Bad secrets are often expected to be kept forever and to conceal something in order to avoid getting someone into trouble.

The Curse of Knowledge

AGE RANGE: 3 to 5 years

RESEARCH AREAS: Cognitive development, theory of mind

 THE EXPERIMENT

On page 248 are three columns. In each column are several images. The topmost image in each set has been obscured by various methods, such as blurring, introduction of noise, or tight cropping. Each subsequent image is slightly less obscured, and the final image shows a clear, unaltered image of a common, recognizable animal or object.

Use sheets of paper to cover all but one of the columns. Then use another sheet of paper to cover all but the topmost image. Explain to your child that you are going to play a guessing game. You will show her an image, and she will try to guess what is pictured. Allow her to try to guess what is pictured in the topmost image. Then, one by one, reveal each of the other images in the set until she is able to correctly guess what object or animal is pictured. Follow the same procedure with the other two image sets, and note at what point your child is able to correctly identify the image.

Now present a stuffed animal or puppet and explain to your child that it's the toy's turn to play the guessing game. Use the sheets of paper to set up the game, so that you are revealing the images from the top down, just as you did before. Tell your child that you want her to say at what point she thinks the stuffed animal recognizes the object shown in the image. Make note of which image in each set she indicates.

 TWEAK IT

Try conducting this same experiment on an adult friend. Rather than having a puppet complete the second part of the experiment, have the adult imagine a same-age peer.

 THE HYPOTHESIS

Your child will expect the toy to be able to recognize the object at an earlier point in the set than she herself was able to identify it. If you also tried the experiment on an adult friend, the same will hold true for him or her.

 THE RESEARCH

A 2004 study recruited preschoolers ages three through five, as well as a group of college students, to participate in an image-recognition task. The participants were individually shown a succession of images on a computer screen that progressed from highly degraded (using alterations such as blurring, noise, or cropping) to not degraded at all. They were asked to identify the point at which they recognized the object pictured. The children were then shown a puppet, Ernie from *Sesame Street*, and the college students were told about a peer named Ernie. The experimenters explained that Ernie was going to do the same image-recognition task. The participants were shown a non-degraded image and were instructed to identify the point during the succession of degraded images at which Ernie should be able to recognize what is pictured.

The results showed that both the preschoolers and the college students exhibited visual hindsight bias, meaning that when they knew the identity of the obscured image ahead of time, they expected others to be able to identify it sooner than they themselves had been able to identify similar images. Or, to put it another way, their mental model of another person's state of mind was biased because of their own knowledge. This held true for all age groups tested, although the effect appears to decline with age.

There are several theories about the underlying mechanism behind hindsight bias. One theory is that people have difficulty preventing their own knowledge from influencing them when they try to reason about what another person might know. Another theory is that we overestimate fluency—the ease with which information comes to mind—when we already know the information. A 2017 study tested the latter theory and found that knowing the answer to a question beforehand affects our opinion about how easily it should come to mind for others. The study concluded that this effect, called fluency misattribution, can indeed cause hindsight bias.

THE TAKEAWAY

The theory of mind is of great interest to cognitive scientists and psychologists. This theory examines what people know about their own and other people's minds, such as the beliefs a person currently holds or the emotions a person is experiencing in the moment. The results of this study suggest that we tend to overestimate another person's perceptual abilities when we have advance knowledge about what this person is trying to perceive. One of the more serious implications of visual hindsight bias relates to eyewitness testimony, because, as the researchers write, "in retrospect, observers tend to believe that viewing conditions at the scene of a crime were better than they actually were." But a more practical takeaway for parents is that this bias can lead both a parent and a child to expect the other to know or understand things before they actually do. The solution to a task in a preschool activity book might seem obvious to you, and that knowledge might lead you to have unrealistic expectations about your child's ability to recognize the solution. Similarly, your child might become frustrated when you prompt her for details about an incident, because she may think that you should be able to understand her thoughts or feelings better than you actually can. But when you are aware of the potential for hindsight bias in your everyday interactions, it will help you be more realistic about your expectations and more understanding when your child is unrealistic in hers.

26 That Ain't Random

AGE RANGE: 3 to 5 years

RESEARCH AREAS: Number sense, statistical thinking

 THE EXPERIMENT

You will need to gather two sets of small manipulative toys or game pieces. The first set, which we will call Set A, should consist of thirty identical objects, such as Lego pieces of the same size and color. The second set, which we will call Set B, should consist of six identical objects, such as clear marbles. You will also need one other small object, such as a pencil eraser, which will act as a control object.

Place all the objects from Set A into a clear bowl on a table, then show your child a puppet or stuffed animal. Explain to your child that the puppet is going to look in the bowl for four things to play with. Then, manipulate the puppet to choose four of the objects from the bowl, and say in the puppet's voice, "Oh, this looks fun!" or "I like this one!" Allow your child to see the puppet playing with the objects for a few moments, and then declare that it is time for the puppet to go away. Place the puppet in your lap, then remove the bowl and all the objects from the table. A few moments later, produce the puppet again and say that it wants to play some more. Place one object from Set A, one object from Set B, and the control object on the table, and say, "Look, it wants to play some more. Can you give it the one that it likes?" Note which of the three objects your child gives to the puppet.

Sometime later, you will repeat this experiment using a different puppet or stuffed animal, but inside the bowl you should place the six objects from Set B and twenty-four objects from Set A. Repeat the experiment, but make sure that the four objects the puppet chooses are from Set B. The puppet should not choose any objects from Set A. Once you have repeated the experiment, note which of the three objects your child gives to the puppet.

 ## THE HYPOTHESIS

When only items from Set A are in the bowl, it's anybody's guess which object your child will select when you prompt him to give the puppet the one that it likes. But when the puppet selects only items from Set B from a container with mostly Set A items, your child is quite likely to select the Set B item when prompted to give the puppet the one that it likes.

It's possible for a person to select from several options without expressing any sort of preference. For instance, you might close your eyes, reach into a box of ping-pong balls of various colors, and pick one at random. It is also possible to have a preference for a particular color of ping-pong ball and to make a deliberate decision based on that preference. In that case, depending on the color distribution of the balls in the box, your selections may look very different from what would be expected if you were picking randomly.

This raises an interesting question. When we observe a decision pattern that looks very different from what we would expect if the decision were made randomly, can we infer that there is some preference or intent behind the choice?

In many cases, we treat it as reasonable to do so.

If, among an employee base in which women outnumber men, a manager selects only male employees for promotion, we might infer that he is expressing a bias. And the more promotions he makes that fit the pattern, the more confident we might feel that our inference is correct.

Researchers in a 2010 study were curious about whether preschool-aged children also employ this statistical principle to infer when a person is expressing a preference.

The children were placed into three groups. Each group watched a puppet select objects from a container, but the contents of the containers were different in each group. In the first group, there was only one type of object. In the second group, there were two types of objects, distributed evenly, and the puppet consistently chose one type over the other. In the third group, there were also two types of objects, but one type, which the puppet consistently chose, made up only about 20 percent of the total. After watching the puppet play with the objects, each child was then presented with both types of objects, along with a novel object used as a control, and asked to select the object that the puppet liked.

The researchers reasoned that if preschoolers infer preferences when they notice a violation of random behavior, then the degree to which the children witnessed such a violation would influence which object they selected as the one that the puppet liked. According to their hypothesis, the children who saw the puppet select from only one type of object would be least likely to infer a preference for that object; those who saw the puppet choose only one type of object from an even distribution would be more likely to infer a preference; and those who saw the puppet choose only one type of object when that object was not very prevalent would be most likely to infer a preference.

Their results showed exactly that. Children in the 20 percent condition were most likely to identify the target object as the one the puppet preferred. Children in the 50 percent condition were slightly less likely, and those in the 100 percent condition were even less likely.

Your child may not even be able to pronounce the word *probability*, but inside that head of his there's a bookmaker weighing the odds and making judgments about the likelihood of all sorts of events.

In the second part of this experiment, in which there were twenty-four items from Set A and six items from Set B, there was only a one-in-five chance of drawing an item from Set B if you were choosing at random. The odds of randomly drawing four items in a row from Set B are 1 in 1,827. Your kid might not be doing the math, but he's definitely recognizing that it's not a likely outcome.

One way that you can help him further develop this skill is by introducing him to new vocabulary words related to probability, such as *certain, uncertain, probable, improbable, possible, impossible, likely,* and *unlikely.* Explain what each word means, offer examples, and ask questions. For instance, you might ask whether it is possible or impossible for a flipped coin to land on heads. Or you might ask whether it is likely or unlikely for a six-sided die to land four-side up. Being able to name and understand these statistical concepts will (probably) help your child learn to articulate what appears to already be a burgeoning intuition about probabilities.

27 **Brain Blocks the Pain**

AGE RANGE: 3 to 5 years

RESEARCH AREAS: Perception, distraction, pain

 THE EXPERIMENT

For this experiment, you'll need a video game that your child can play one-handed. You might use an app on a tablet or a phone, or a gaming system with a joystick. You'll also need to fill a large bowl with chilly water. It should be around 50 degrees Fahrenheit (10 degrees Celsius). Finally, you'll need a stopwatch for keeping time.

Invite your child to complete a chilly challenge. Explain that the challenge involves seeing how long she can keep her hand in cold water. Make sure she understands that she does not need to complete the challenge if she does not want to, and that she can withdraw her hand anytime she wants.

If she agrees, direct her to place her unclenched, nondominant hand wrist-deep into the chilly water and keep it there for as long as she can stand it. Use the stopwatch to time her performance, from the moment her hand is submerged to when she withdraws it. Write down her time. We'll call this the baseline score.

Next, invite her to complete the same challenge while watching a TV show, and write down her time again. We'll call this the passive distraction score. Finally, invite her to complete the challenge one more time, but while playing the video game with her other hand. Write down her time for this third attempt. We'll call this the active distraction score.

If, during any of the three trials, she keeps her hand in for more than four minutes, you can stop the trial. Be sure to warm your child's hand fully after each trial.

 THE HYPOTHESIS

Your child will keep her hand in the cold water longer during each of the distraction conditions than during the baseline condition.

THE RESEARCH

A cold pressor test involves submerging one's hand in icy water for as long as one can bear it. It's a tool that psychologists use to study people's tolerance for pain and how that tolerance can be experimentally manipulated.

Children in a 2011 study participated in a series of cold pressor challenges. Each child completed at least one baseline test, during which they did not engage in any distracting tasks. Then, they were randomly assigned to either an active or a passive distraction group. The children in the active distraction group played a video game with their dominant hand, and the children in the passive distraction group watched a video recording of game play.

The results showed that for baseline trials, most children kept their hands submerged for eight to twenty-four seconds, with a median time of about fourteen seconds. For the distraction trials, most children kept their hands submerged for at least a few extra seconds compared with the baseline; the median time for the active distraction trial was about eighteen seconds, and the median time for the passive distraction trial was about twenty-two seconds.

The researchers highlighted one notable difference between the results of this study, which involved children between ages three and five, and an earlier 2007 study in which children ages five to thirteen completed the same types of trials. The 2007 study had found that active distractions were more effective than passive distractions, whereas the study focusing on preschoolers found no significant difference in their effects.

 **THE TAKEAWAY**

It's very common for young children to express some fear and anxiety about routine vaccinations and blood work, as well as other medical procedures that involve pain or discomfort. Heck, even pulling off an especially sticky bandage can sometimes lead to tears. The results of this study, however, show that playing a video game, or even watching a video game being played, can be useful in managing pain in young children. One other way to help distract your child during needle sticks is to use a Shot-Blocker. This inexpensive plastic device has small bumps on one side, and when it's pressed against the skin surrounding the injection site, your child is more likely to notice the feeling of the bumps and less likely to notice the pain from the needle prick. For extra distraction, combine the device with a game of *Tetris*.

28 A Strange Sort

AGE RANGE: 3 to 5 years

RESEARCH AREA: Cognitive development

 THE EXPERIMENT

Photocopy and cut out the twelve cards that accompany this project (page 249). On half of the cards, there is a triangle shape, and on the other half, there is a circle shape. For each shape, half of the cards are shaded and the other half are unshaded.

Have your child sit at a table and show him the cards. Point out that some of the cards have triangles, while others have circles. Also point out that some of the cards are shaded, while other cards are unshaded.

Shuffle the cards and place them in a pile in front of him. Explain that you are going to play a shape-sorting game, and his job is to sort the cards into two piles by shape. Tell him to place all the triangle cards in a pile at his left and all the circle cards in a pile at his right. After he has sorted eight of the twelve cards, interrupt him and explain that now the sorting rules are going to change. Shaded cards should go in the pile at his left, and unshaded cards should go in the pile to his right.

Allow him to complete the sorting task with the remaining cards, and pay attention to whether he continues sorting according to the first rule or adapts to the new rule.

 ## THE HYPOTHESIS

At three years old, your child is likely to continue sorting the cards according to the first rule. Four- and five-year-olds are increasingly less likely to make this error.

 ## THE RESEARCH

Children in a 2005 study were asked to complete a card-sorting task in which the rules shifted midway through the exercise. One of the trials used a deck of cards consisting of green cars and orange flowers. The children were first directed to sort the cards by their shape, and then directed to sort the cards by their color.

The researchers found that many of the children, particularly the younger ones, exhibited what psychologists call a perseverative error, meaning they continued to repeat the behavior they had learned initially and failed to adapt to the transition. This type of error is common in young children and has been documented in a wide variety of experiments. For example, in one famous experiment babies played a simplified version of a shell game, in which a toy was placed into one of two containers, and they had to reach in and find the toy. After repeated trials, the toy was conspicuously moved to the other container, but many babies continued to reach into the original container.

One new thing that the 2005 study revealed was that if the experimenter gently corrected a child who had made such an error, the child generally tended to sort the rest of the cards according to the new rule. This suggests that the perseverative error, at least in this case, is not a result of the children being unable to absorb the new information. Rather, it's a result of failing to transition their activity when they acquire the new information. And a gentle correction seems to be enough to help the children refocus their attention and fully make the transition.

 **THE TAKEAWAY**

Your child's ability to follow rule-based instructions is still developing, and he may struggle to adapt to changes to those rules, especially if he has become habituated to the old way of doing things. For instance, his normal volume level probably ranges from slightly loud to drunken-sailor loud. If you take him to a library, where he is expected to speak at a lower volume, he may fail to comply with that expectation, even after being given instructions ahead of time to use a quiet voice. Take heart, though. The results of this research suggest that a gentle correction is typically enough to help your child remember that new rules are in effect. Granted, you may need to correct him a dozen times during the course of the library trip, but after each reminder you should see attempts at compliance.

Who Knows Best?

AGE RANGE: 3 to 5 years

RESEARCH AREAS: Social development, trust

 THE EXPERIMENT

In this experiment, you'll tell a story about two girls with different personalities. Draw a stick figure to represent each of the girls: one stick figure should have a smiling face and one should have a frowning face. Then, gather an opaque container and two small objects, each of which can be concealed in the container. The objects should be familiar to your child, and she should be able to recognize each of them by its name.

Introduce the first stick figure to your child and explain that her name is Jamie, and she is a very kind girl who often does nice things for people. For instance, at school when she sees a kid carrying a heavy load of books, she offers to help carry some of the books. Then, introduce the second stick figure and explain that her name is Virginia, and she is not a very kind girl and often does mean things. For instance, at school when she sees a kid carrying a heavy load of books, she bumps into him and makes the books fall on the ground!

Out of your child's sight, place one of the familiar objects into the container. Then, explain to your child that there is an object inside the container, and that Jamie and Virginia are both going to peek to see what's inside. Allow your child to see the stick figures look inside the container, and then ask her which of the characters she wants to ask about what's inside. Regardless of which character she chooses, have Jamie, the kind character, indicate the correct name for the object, and have Virginia, the mean character, indicate an incorrect name for the object. Ask your child which of the two names identifies the object in the container. Then, reveal the object.

Again out of your child's sight, place the other familiar object in the container. Then, explain that there is another object inside the container, different from the first, and Virginia is going to peek at it. Allow your child to see the stick figure of Virginia peek inside the container. Now both characters should say what they think is inside the container. Have Jamie, the kind character, indicate an incorrect name for the object, and have Virginia, the mean character, indicate the correct name. Ask your child which of the two names identifies the object in the container. Then, reveal the object.

THE HYPOTHESIS

When the first object is hidden inside the container and both characters get to peek at it, your child is likely to say that she would rather ask Jamie than Virginia about what's inside, and she's likely to trust Jamie's assertion about the object's name more than Virginia's. When the second object is hidden inside the container and only the mean character gets to peek at it, your preschooler is still likely to say that she would rather ask Jamie than Virginia about what's inside, and she's still likely to trust Jamie's assertion about the object's name more than Virginia's, even though it was Virginia and not Jaime who got to peek at the object.

THE RESEARCH

Children in a 2013 study were introduced to pairs of characters. One of the characters had a desirable trait, such as being smart, kind, or honest, while the other character had a corresponding undesirable trait, such as being stupid, mean, or dishonest. They were then shown a box with a concealed object inside, and both characters were shown peeking into the box. The children were asked which character they would prefer to ask about the contents of the box, and when both characters offered an answer, the children selected which answer they trusted more. Next, the character with the undesirable trait peeked into another box, while the other character did not. The children were asked again which character they would prefer to ask about the contents of the box, and when both characters offered an answer, the children selected which answer they trusted more.

The researchers found that in the case in which each character peeked inside the box, children strongly preferred to ask the character with the desirable trait, and trusted that character's answer more than that of the character with the undesirable trait. In the case in which only the character with the undesirable trait peeked inside the box, children under age five nevertheless tended to put more trust in the answer offered by the character with the desirable trait, even though that character did not get to see inside the box. (Children between ages five and seven, on the other hand, tended to put more trust in the character who got a peek inside.)

The results suggest that preschoolers tend to attribute knowledge to characters with positive traits and a lack of knowledge to characters with negative traits, even in situations in which they would readily pick up on which characters possessed the necessary knowledge if the characters each had neutral traits.

And it's not only traits related to character that influence children's trust. A 2014 study found that children tend to put more trust in people if they are physically attractive.

THE TAKEAWAY

Learning who can be trusted to provide accurate information can be a complicated task, not only for young children but also for adults. Typically, we gauge a person's knowledge and trustworthiness based on multiple factors, such as previous interactions and inferences. For instance, we might ask, "How often have they provided inaccurate information in the past?" or "What do I know about what they could know?" But a number of biases creep into our reasoning as well. The results of this study show that for preschoolers, positive traits are not only a bias but also potentially a blinder, causing them to reach exactly the opposite conclusion that they might reach if the traits weren't a factor. Because of this, it's especially important to emphasize to your child that just because a person is friendly or nice or good-looking does not mean they know it all, or that they can be trusted without reservation. Even someone who is generally smart can make some really magnificent blunders sometimes, so encourage your child to take a step back, think critically, and not allow a person's charm or admirable qualities distort reality.

Pretzel Logic

AGE RANGE: 3 to 5 years

RESEARCH AREA: Decision making

THE EXPERIMENT

There are two stages in this experiment. Both involve salty pretzels, water, and a simple game, such as marbles, jacks, or dominoes.

In the first stage, select an engaging book that takes about ten minutes to read, and present a bowl of pretzels to your child. Tell him he is allowed to eat as many of the pretzels as he would like during the story. Once you have finished reading the story, present the game and explain that on the following day, your child will have a chance to play this game with you. Ask him, "What would you like to have tomorrow while playing the game: some pretzels to eat, or some water to drink?" Note your child's choice, then offer him some water. (He'll probably be thirsty after eating all those pretzels.) On the following day, follow through by playing the game with him and offering him whichever option he selected.

In the second stage, which should take place a week or more later, you will again read a ten-minute story to your child, but this time, don't offer him anything to eat or drink while he's following along. After the story is complete, present the game again and explain that on the following day, he will have a chance to play the game with you. Ask the same question you asked before: "What would you like to have tomorrow while playing the game: some pretzels to eat, or some water to drink?" Note your child's choice, and make sure to follow through with the game on the next day.

 ## THE HYPOTHESIS

During the first stage, your child is likely to request water, rather than pretzels, for the next day's activity. But during the second stage, he is likely to request pretzels.

 ## THE RESEARCH

In a 2006 study, preschoolers were split into groups. One group was offered salty pretzels to snack on during a story, while another group listened to the story without a snack. The children were then told that they would be playing a marble game on the following day and were asked which they would prefer to have during the game: pretzels or water.

The children who had not snacked during story time showed a strong preference for pretzels over water. The children who had loaded up on pretzels, however, showed a strong preference for water over pretzels, even though they understood that they would be receiving their choice the next day, when, presumably, they would not be feeling quite so thirsty.

The researchers concluded that preschool-aged children allow their future preferences to be heavily influenced by their current desires. The kids who were thirsty from eating a salty snack made choices that corresponded to what they were feeling in the present. They appeared not to take into account that they might not be feeling quite so thirsty the next day. Even the children in the group that had not snacked during story time were expressing a preference consistent with their current desires. The researchers confirmed this by repeating the experiment with a separate group of children who got to have their choice right away, rather than having to wait until the next day. Children in that group expressed a preference for pretzels as well, suggesting that kids tend to prefer pretzels over a glass of water—except when they're feeling parched.

 **THE TAKEAWAY**

You and your child may not be as different as you think when it comes to allowing present desires to influence our choices about the future. After all, you've probably succumbed to an impulse purchase, thinking that you will desire the item at a later date, and later experienced buyer's remorse. Even so, you probably have more intuition and self-control than your child, so it's important to help him understand that just because you desire something now doesn't mean you'll have the same desire for it at a later time. And it's important for you to keep his bias toward present desires in mind. If you ask your child in the summer what he'd like for a winter birthday present, for instance, he might only be able to think about warm-weather toys that would be of no use during the colder months. One way to help him think more clearly about the future is to help him visualize it. Prompt him to imagine being bundled up in a snowsuit and crunching through new-fallen snow. That might help him get into the right frame of mind to request a sled rather than a boogie board.

Share What's Fair

AGE RANGE: 3 to 5 years

RESEARCH AREAS: Social development, sharing, fairness

THE EXPERIMENT

You'll need two relatively large teddy bears or other stuffed animals, along with an assortment of twelve smaller toys. You'll also need a helper, with whom you will act out the teddy bears' parts.

Have your child sit between the two bears, and distribute four toys to each animal and four toys to your child. Let your child play with the toys. Meanwhile, you and the helper should allow each bear to play with the toys they were given. After about a minute, collect all the toys and explain that you are going to redistribute them. Give three toys to your child and nine toys to the bear that your helper has control of. Explain that everyone can begin playing with the toys again.

Now do some playacting with your bear, and stop the experiment once your child responds. First, say, "I don't have any toys." Note whether your child responds in some way, such as by offering some of her own toys or by suggesting that the other bear share its toys. If, after a few seconds' pause, your child has not responded, have the bear say, "I wish I had toys to play with." Again, note whether your child responds. If not, after another pause, have your bear reach in your child's direction. If, after a final pause, your child still has not responded, have the bear directly ask your child, "May I please have some of your toys?"

 ## THE HYPOTHESIS

Both three-year-olds and five-year-olds are more likely to share some of their own toys than to appeal to the other bear. But five-year-olds will be more likely than three-year-olds to involve the bear who has the most toys, such as by asking that bear to share with the other bear.

 ## THE RESEARCH

In a 2013 study on sharing, researchers had children ages three and five sit at table. Two stuffed bears were seated nearby. At first, the experimenters distributed an equal number of toys to the child and each bear. Then, the toys were gathered up and distributed unequally. The child received a quarter of the toys, one of the bears received the rest of the toys, and the other bear received none. The bear who received no toys then began to appeal, in increasingly direct ways, for the child to share. The researchers took note of whether the child refused to share, agreed to share some or all of the toys, or appealed to the other bear to share its toys.

In about half of all trials, children in both the three-year-old group and the five-year-old group agreed to share some of their toys. On average, they shared about half of their toys. Three-year-olds were very unlikely to involve the other bear. Five-year-olds were more likely to ask the other bear to share its toys, although not as likely as they were to share their own toys. In a follow-up experiment in which the child, rather than the other bear, was given the majority of the toys, five-year-olds were more likely to share their own toys than in the previous experiment, and less likely to involve the bear with the smaller number of toys.

The researchers concluded that at both ages three and five, children were sensitive to the unequal distribution of toys and were willing to act, either by sharing their own toys or by appealing to the other bear to share its toys, to make the distribution more equal. But differences emerged in their expectations about the fairest way to resolve inequality. Three-year-olds generally did not involve the bear with the most resources; the few who did just reached over and took its toys, rather than appealing to the bear's sense of fairness. In contrast, five-year-olds appeared sensitive to which participant had the most resources. When it was the other bear, their appeals typically made mention of that fact, and when the children had the majority of the toys, it increased their likelihood of sharing.

THE TAKEAWAY

Fairness is an extremely important concept to preschoolers, and most will very vocally object when they observe unfairness, especially when it's at their own expense. The results of this study suggest that between ages three and five, your child's innate sense of fairness becomes more developed. Children become more willing to socially engage with others and to encourage others to share their resources when they have more than their fair share. It bears noting that the reason why they make these appeals is because they have come to understand that fairness is a moral concept that is recognized by nearly all people, that one's duty to share becomes greater with the amount of resources they have, and that by appealing to another person's sense of duty, they can persuade that person to share. These are sophisticated concepts. Problems that involve equitable distribution of resources might, in fact, be the first time that your child has to confront both math and morality together.

One way to encourage your child to share is by helping her develop empathy. You might, for instance, ask your child how she would feel if she were the bear with no toys. Does the lack of toys feel even more painful when others have many toys but are unwilling to share? As your child develops a greater sensitivity to inequality, she is likely to expect others to have a similar sensitivity and may become frustrated when they refuse to share or when they act callously. Emphasize to your child that although she might not be able to compel others to share, setting a good example is always an appropriate way to positively influence them.

32 O, Really!

AGE RANGE: 3 to 5 years

RESEARCH AREAS: Writing, language development

THE EXPERIMENT

Give your child a sheet of paper and a pencil. Ask him to write the following letters, without looking at them: A, B, K, O, T. Note whether your child is able to write each letter.

THE HYPOTHESIS

Three-year-olds will probably not be able to write any of the five letters, but if they do correctly write a letter, it will almost assuredly be the letter O. Four-year-olds are unlikely to be able to write a K (unless it's part of their name), but they have a decent shot at being able to write the other letters, and they are most likely to be able to write an O. Five-year-olds are likely to perform even better with all five letters, and they, too, will have the best chance of success with the letter O.

 ## THE RESEARCH

In a 2011 study that examined preschoolers' burgeoning written-language skills, participants were given a battery of writing tasks, the most basic of which involved writing letters of the alphabet. Three-year-olds were generally unable to write any of the letters, with the exception of the letter O—although even in that case, only about 40 percent were successful. Four-year-olds showed considerable progress. More than half of them were able to write the letters A, B, O, and T. The letter K was relatively difficult for them; only about a third wrote it successfully. By age five, about three quarters of the children were able to write the easier letters, but K remained difficult, with fewer than half of the participants able to write it successfully.

What makes a particular letter more or less difficult to write? The letter O involves a single stroke, in a shape your child has probably had opportunities to practice outside of letter writing, and it is recognizable as an O even if the shape formed is somewhat oblong or jittery. The letter T is also relatively simple to write and occurs relatively frequently in the English language.

While more complicated to write, the letters A and B occupy the starting positions in the alphabet, so your child is likely to be familiar with them. Poor letter K has none of these qualities. It occurs with less frequency relative to the other letters, it's almost in the middle of the alphabet, and it involves three strokes, whose points of intersection can be tricky to get right. No wonder it's a tough one, even for kids who have mastered other letters.

That said, if the letter K happens to be part of your child's name, there's a good chance it will be among the letters he can write. Often, a child's name is the first word he learns to write, and children tend to be familiar with the letters of their own name even if those letters are otherwise uncommon. In fact, a 2003 study found that name writing is such a key factor in early writing that it can predict a child's score on many other indicators of emerging literacy, such as knowledge of the alphabet, conceptualization of the written word, and rhyme awareness. And a 2012 study found that the association between name-writing ability and other measures of emerging literacy hold true regardless of the number of letters in a child's name, so whether your child is a Bo or a Bartholomew, a Jo or a Josephine, name-writing proficiency will generally be an indicator of developing literacy skills.

THE TAKEAWAY

Regardless of where your child is now in his letter-writing or name-writing ability, it is likely that his progression from scribbles to proper penmanship will involve a years-long process with varying stages of growth. If your child is not yet able to write any letters, don't fret. Even making letter-like scribbles is a footstep on the path to literacy, so encourage your child when he pretends to write. If he is able to write a handful of letters, such as those in his own name, consider whether there are any similarly shaped letters that you could encourage him to try to master next. If your child has already learned to write the majority of letters in the alphabet, there are many avenues you can pursue to help bolster early literacy skills, such as strengthening penmanship for the letters he can already write, exploring how to write the remaining letters, and stringing together letters to form words.

Keep in mind that some children develop these skills earlier than others, and the various skills that contribute to writing and reading ability can develop more or less rapidly compared with each other, so your child may experience bursts of insights or improvements, or may take a slow and winding road toward literacy.

㉝ Taught or Not

AGE RANGE: 3 to 5 years

RESEARCH AREAS: Perception, intentionality

 THE EXPERIMENT

Following are four short stories that involve children acquiring, or failing to acquire, a new skill. Read each of the four stories to your child, then ask the questions that follow the story and note your child's responses. You can present all four stories at once, or at different times over the course of a day, or even on separate days.

STORY 1

Steve and Donna are friends. Steve does not know how to button a jacket. Donna does know how to button a jacket. Each day,

Donna shows Steve how to button a jacket. She says, "Look, find the buttonhole that matches each button, and push the button through the hole." Each day, Donna shows Steve how to fasten the buttons. Now Steve knows how to button a jacket.

QUESTION SET 1

- At the beginning, did Steve know how to button a jacket?

- Does Steve now know how to button a jacket?

- Did Donna try to teach Steve how to button a jacket?

STORY 2

Renee and Brett are friends. Renee does not know how to tie her shoes. Brett does know how to tie his shoes. Each day, Renee watches Brett as he ties his shoes. She sits nearby, watches how he ties them, and tries to do the same things he does. Brett does not know that Renee is watching him, because she sits behind him. After a while, Renee has learned to tie her shoes just like Brett.

QUESTION SET 2

- At the beginning, did Renee know how to tie her shoes?

- Does Renee now know how to tie her shoes?

- Did Brett know that Renee was watching him tie his shoes?

- Did Brett try to teach Renee how to tie her shoes?

STORY 3

Sarah and Zack are friends. Sarah does not know how to play marbles. Zack does know how to play marbles. He says, "Look, you put the marbles inside a circle, then you flick a big marble, called a shooter, into the circle, and you get points for any marbles you knock out." Sarah tries and tries to play marbles, but she still does not know how.

QUESTION SET 3

- At the beginning, did Sarah know how to play marbles?

- Does Sarah now know how to play marbles?

- Did Zack try to teach Sarah how to play marbles?

STORY 4

Chad and Lauren are friends. Chad does not know how to hop on one foot. Lauren does know how to hop on one foot. Each day at recess, Chad watches as Lauren hops on one foot. He stands by a door behind her and watches her, and he tries to do what she does. Lauren does not know that Chad is watching her. Chad tries over and over to jump on one foot, but he still does not know how to do it.

- At the beginning, did Chad know how to hop on one foot?

- Does Chad now know how to hop on one foot?

- Did Lauren know that Chad was watching her hop on one foot?

- Did Lauren try to teach Chad how to hop on one foot?

 THE HYPOTHESIS

At three and four years old, your child is likely to mistakenly indicate that failed teaching is not teaching at all, and to confuse successful imitation with teaching. By five years old, however, your child is likely to be able to distinguish between teaching and imitation, regardless of whether the teaching or imitation is successful.

 THE RESEARCH

Children in a 2008 study were read a series of stories. Some of the stories depicted intentional teaching of a skill, while others described imitative attempts that did not involve intentional teaching. The children were quizzed after each story about whether the subject of the story was successfully able to acquire the new skill and whether he or she was taught that skill by another person.

When a story described a child being taught a skill and successfully acquiring the skill, children in all age groups were able to correctly identify it as an instance of intentional teaching. But when a story described a child being taught a skill and being unsuccessful at acquiring the skill, three- and four-year-olds had trouble identifying it as an instance of intentional teaching. Only about 40 percent of three-year-olds and 60 percent of four-year-olds were able to do so. Five-year-olds, on the other hand, had no trouble identifying these failed attempts as teaching.

Likewise, when a story described a child covertly observing and imitating another child and failing to successfully imitate that child, children of all ages agreed that this was not an instance of teaching. However, when the attempts at imitation were successful, three- and four-year-olds had difficulty differentiating that from teaching. About 80 percent of three-year-olds and 70 percent of four-year-olds incorrectly said that the child who acquired the skill had been taught, whereas only 20 percent of five-year-olds made that error.

The researchers concluded that younger children tend to judge whether instruction has taken place by the outcome, but by about five years old, children tend to have discovered that teaching requires intentionality.

What does it matter whether your child is able to recognize that teaching is an intentional action? Sure, it's nice that she can distinguish between instruction and imitation, but what practical implications does it have? Turns out, being able to recognize when teaching is occurring can help your child better cooperate with the process. For instance, if a child is playing an educational game, she may begin to recognize the didactic elements of the game and come to see the game in a new light, recognizing its purpose, rather than just its rules. Similarly, if a teacher asks, "When ice melts, what does it become?" a younger child may interpret the question as merely a request for information, but a child with a more developed intuition about instruction may recognize that the teacher is asking the question not because she doesn't know the answer, but because she wants to test the child's knowledge. And understanding the teacher's purpose helps your child become more receptive to what is being taught.

In your day-to-day interactions with your child, you can help correct any mistaken assumptions about what it means to be taught something and what it means to learn something. Point out that it is possible to learn something without having been intentionally taught, as when we imitate someone else's behavior. On the flip side, it is possible to be taught something even if we don't learn it immediately, because teaching is a choice on the part of the instructor to share knowledge with someone.

Whether the person learns the information is another story. When you help your child understand these distinctions, you teach her about what it means to be taught. It's a bit of a mind bender, but by five years old, your child is probably ready to wrap her head around it.

③④ Get a Grip

AGE RANGE: 3 to 5 years

RESEARCH AREAS: Motor skills, planning

 THE EXPERIMENT

You'll need a thin cardboard tube, two cardboard boxes of the same height, and a third, smaller cardboard box. Wrap and paste a sheet of colored construction paper around half of the tube. Cut a small hole in the top of the third box that is just large enough for the tube to fit through. When the tube is placed in the hole, it should stand upright.

For the first part of the experiment, place the two same-size cardboard boxes across from each other on a table so the tube, with its colored portion on the right, rests on top of them and forms a bridge. Place the other box nearby, with the hole facing up. Instruct your child to pick up the tube with her right hand and place it into the hole so that the colored part of the tube goes in the hole first. Observe whether she uses an overhand or underhand grip to pick up the tube and maneuver it into the hole.

The second part of the experiment begins just as the first does. The tube should rest on top of the two equal-height boxes, with its colored portion on the right. The other box should again rest nearby, with the hole facing up. This time, however, instruct your child to pick up the tube with her right hand and place it into the hole so that the *uncolored* part of the tube goes in the hole first. Again, note whether she uses an overhand or underhand grip to complete the maneuver.

 THE HYPOTHESIS

For the first part of the experiment, in which the colored end of the tube goes in the hole first, your child is very likely to use an overhand grip, which allows her right hand to end in a comfortable position once the tube is inserted. For the second part, the grip she chooses is likely to depend on her age. Three-year-olds are unlikely to use an underhand grip, even though it would allow their hand to end in the most comfortable position. Four-year-olds are about as likely as not to use an underhand grip, and five-year-olds are more likely to choose an underhand grip.

If you've ever had to move heavy furniture through a narrow space, you've probably learned that it's wise to anticipate the movements you will need to make. This allows you to make sure you can hold the furniture in the most comfortable position and avoid orienting yourself or the furniture in a way that causes difficulty in moving through the space. When it comes to reaching for objects, adults tend to plan ahead and figure out the method of reaching that will result in the most comfortable ending position. (Think about how you reach for an overturned glass.)

Researchers in a 2010 study were curious about when children begin to adjust their grip in a way that anticipates end-state comfort. They presented three-, four-, and five-year-old children with a task in which a dual-colored wooden dowel could be picked up and placed in a holder with either an overhand or an underhand grip. In cases in which an overhand grip resulted in the most comfortable end-state position of their hands, all of the children chose that type of grip. But in cases in which an underhand grip resulted in the most comfortable end-state position, there were noticeable age-related differences. Less than 20 percent of three-year-olds used an underhand grip, whereas nearly half of four-year-olds and 70 percent of five-year-olds opted for underhand.

The researchers concluded that anticipatory planning of mo-

tor movements appears to be something that develops notice-
ably during the preschool years. However, they also noted that
when the youngest group of children engaged in a second and
third trial, at least a small contingent of them began switching to
an underhand grip when that resulted in better end-state comfort, so it may be the case that practice can help hurry along this
aspect of development.

 THE TAKEAWAY

Being able to plan ahead and make choices that are temporarily
uncomfortable but lead to increased comfort later involves a rich
set of skills that develops throughout childhood and early adult-
hood. Sometimes, children fail to exercise the self-control necessary to put aside comfort in the present in exchange for a future
payoff. But in other cases, they may fail to plan ahead simply
because they don't know how to predict what will happen next.
In this experiment, even if your child can plan the motions necessary to accomplish the task, she might not be able to predict
how her hand will feel as she's carrying out those motions. But
the results of this study show that repetition and practice can
help a child acquire that knowledge and use it to plan future
movements.

Shelving It

Another test designed to measure whether participants plan their movements to maximize end-state comfort is called the grasp height task. A vertical cylinder is placed on a bookcase that has multiple shelves, and participants must pick up the cylinder and move it to a different shelf. The test was first used in a 2004 study, which found that adult participants grasped the cylinder at a lower position when they needed to move it to a higher shelf and at a higher position when they needed to move it to a lower shelf. These grasping positions help the participants maximize their end-state comfort.

Researchers in a 2017 study gave the grasp height task to children ages three to five. As with the adults in the previous study, the children adjusted the height at which they grasped the cylinder based on the height of the shelf to which it was being moved, indicating that they were taking end-state comfort into account. Compared with the procedure and required movements described in "Get a Grip," moving items up and down on a shelf is simpler for children to reason through and execute, which might explain why the end-state comfort effect was seen among three-year-olds in this study, but not in the 2010 study involving wooden dowels.

35 Tailored Teaching

AGE RANGE: 3 to 5 years

RESEARCH AREAS: Cognitive development, teaching

THE EXPERIMENT

Gather the following items: two small square pieces of construction paper, one red and one a different color; some tape; a small magnet; a small nonmagnetic item; and four stuffed animals. Tape the squares of construction paper side by side to a refrigerator or other metallic surface.

Explain to your child that you are going to teach her a simple game, and then she'll get a chance to watch some stuffed animals play the game. Read the following instructions on how to play:

There are two squares here, side by side. One is red and one is not. There are also two game pieces here. One is a magnet and will stick

to the fridge, and one is not a magnet and will not stick to the
fridge. There are two rules to the game: You have to put a game
piece on the red square, and it has to stay stuck to the square. When
you place a game piece on the red square and it stays stuck to the
square, you win the game!

Now present the four stuffed animals and explain that they were each taught the rules of the game, but they might make mistakes.

Manipulate the first stuffed animal so it selects the nonmagnetic piece and places it on the non-red square. When the piece is released, it will fall to the floor. Then, ask your child whether the stuffed animal played the game correctly. Also ask whether it understood all of the rules, some of the rules, or none of the rules. Now prompt your child to teach the stuffed animal so it can play the game better, and note whether your child teaches by showing or telling the stuffed animal the correct way to play.

Next, repeat the same procedure with the second stuffed animal, only manipulate it so it selects the nonmagnetic piece and places it on the red square. Then ask your child the same questions and prompt her to teach the toy to play better.

Repeat the procedure for the third stuffed animal, except that it should select the magnetic game piece but place it on the non-red square. Again, ask your child the same questions and prompt her to teach the toy to play better.

Finally, repeat the procedure once more with the fourth stuffed animal, except that it should select the magnetic game piece and place it on the red square. (Because this stuffed animal wins the game, there is no need for your child to teach it how to play better.)

 THE HYPOTHESIS

Your child is likely to be able to identify that the fourth stuffed animal, who made no mistakes, played the game correctly, and that the other three, who made at least one mistake each, did not play the game correctly. But she is unlikely to be able to correctly identify which of the four players understood all of the rules, which understood only some, and which did not understand any of the rules.

Additionally, the methods your child uses to teach the stuffed animals may differ, depending on her age. Three-year-olds are about twice as likely to show than tell; four-year-olds are equally likely to show or tell; and five-year-olds are about twice as likely to tell than show. Five-year-olds are also much more likely than younger children to use contrasting language, such as by pointing out the incorrect behavior and then explaining the correct behavior.

 THE RESEARCH

A 2016 study of children between ages three and five involved teaching them a game similar to the one you taught your child, then having each child observe some puppets play the game. One puppet violated both rules (the rule about where to place the game piece and the rule about the game piece having to stick to the surface). Two other puppets violated one rule each. And a fourth puppet played the game correctly. The children were then quizzed about how well each puppet played the game and were given an opportunity to teach the puppets who made errors.

The researchers found that all of the children were able to identify that the puppet who made two errors did not play the game correctly and that the puppet who made no errors did play the game correctly. Practically all of the children were able to identify that the two puppets who made one error each did not play the game correctly. But when the children had to identify which players understood all, some, or none of the rules, hardly any children under age five gave the correct answers for all four puppets, and even among five-year-olds, only about a quarter of them answered correctly for all four puppets.

As for the children's teaching styles, the use of showing rather than telling decreased with age, and older children were more likely to present contrasting information. Five-year-olds were also more likely than younger children to tailor their instruction to the specific mistake a puppet made. For instance, if a puppet placed a magnetic game piece on the wrong-color square, a tailored response would be "You have to put it on the *red* square." About half of the five-year-olds gave a tailored response in at least one of the two cases in which a puppet followed one, but not both, rules.

The researchers concluded that by about five years old, children begin to develop the ability to understand the extent of another person's knowledge based on their behavior and to adapt their instruction accordingly, which is a key skill required to efficiently communicate about complex ideas.

THE TAKEAWAY

"Show, don't tell" might be good advice if your child is writing the next great novel, but when it comes to instruction, being able to use her verbal abilities, rather than just demonstrating the correct course of action, allows her to easily communicate extra information, such as contrasting an incorrect approach with a correct approach. In this simple game, a lack of verbal skills might not be a huge impediment, but it can be difficult to teach the rules of a more complicated game, such as chess, through demonstration alone. You can help your child hone her teaching skills by inviting her to teach a game to a sibling or friend and by giving her hints, if necessary, about how to tailor her approach so that she only needs to spend time teaching things the other person doesn't know. It's often observed that children learn well by teaching others, so your child can share what she knows and perhaps strengthen her own skills in the process.

㊱ Fishing for Prizes

AGE RANGE: 3 to 5 years

RESEARCH AREAS: Cognitive development, problem solving, tool use

 THE EXPERIMENT

You will need three pipe cleaners, a pencil, a tall cup, a plastic bottle cap, some tape, and a small sticker. Construct a "bucket" by bending a pipe cleaner into a handle and taping it to the bottle cap. Place the sticker in the bucket, and place the bucket in the cup.

Present a straight pipe cleaner to your child and explain that his mission is to use it to retrieve the bucket from the cup and earn the sticker as a reward. Give him about one minute to try to use the pipe cleaner to retrieve the bucket and note whether he is successful.

If he is not able to use the pipe cleaner successfully, produce the third pipe cleaner, say, "Watch this," and then silently demonstrate how you can curl the pipe cleaner around a pencil. After your demonstration, give him another minute to try to fish the bucket out of the cup with his pipe cleaner.

If he is still not able to use the pipe cleaner successfully, produce the third pipe cleaner again, say, "Watch this," and silently demonstrate how the end of the pipe cleaner can be curled to form a hook. After this final demonstration, give him one more minute to try to retrieve the bucket.

 THE HYPOTHESIS

Your child is unlikely to spontaneously make a hook with his pipe cleaner either before or after seeing you curl the pipe cleaner around the pencil. But after seeing you demonstrate how to make a hook, he is likely to copy your technique and use the hook he has fashioned to successfully retrieve the bucket.

 THE RESEARCH

In a 2011 study of tool creation and tool use in young children, participants were given a straight pipe cleaner and encouraged to retrieve a small "bucket" from inside a tube. Among children ages three and four, very few managed to spontaneously fashion the pipe cleaner into a tool that could retrieve the bucket, and only about a third of five-year-olds did so. But after an adult experimenter demonstrated how to make a hook, nearly every participant was able to imitate it and complete the task.

The researchers thought maybe the children didn't realize that a pipe cleaner could be bent, or didn't think that bending pipe cleaners was permitted. So, in a follow-up experiment, they included a step in which an experimenter showed the children how a pipe cleaner could be wrapped around a pen. Nevertheless, even after observing that the pipe cleaner was bendable, the children struggled to spontaneously create a hook. One other experiment presented children with both a straight pipe cleaner and a hooked pipe cleaner and allowed them to select which one they wanted to use to try to retrieve the bucket. Children in all age groups chose the hooked pipe cleaner more often. The researchers concluded that tool use, and in particular the ability to select the best tool for a job, is a skill that children develop well before tool creation.

 **THE TAKEAWAY**

Not everyone has the MacGyver-like ability to fashion a tool out of whatever odds and ends are at hand, but most adults do have some aptitude for making changes to existing tools to adapt them to new uses. In a pinch, you might use a wire coat hanger to unclog a drain or use a belt buckle as a bottle opener. Yet even though children innovate through imaginative play and artistic works, creating new tools appears to be a dim spot in their development, at least during their preschool years. It doesn't have to be a significant obstacle to their daily lives, though. By demonstrating new uses for existing items, you may not be able to immediately turn your child into a prodigious inventor, but you can at least help him become more familiar with the idea that new tools can be made from existing items. And sometimes a kid doesn't need to know the ins and outs of material science or engineering processes; he just needs to see you make a hook so he can imitate you and capture a sticker.

37 Of Pigeons and Preschoolers

AGE RANGE: 3 to 5 years

RESEARCH AREA: Decision making

THE EXPERIMENT

You will present to your child a version of the classic Monty Hall problem. On an index card, draw a smiling face. On two other index cards, draw frowning faces. Cut out three cardboard rectangles that are about double the size of the cards and place them side by side on a table opposite your child.

Show the three cards to her and explain that you are going to play a game in which the object is to find the card with the smiling face. If she finds that card, she wins that round of the game, and if she finds one of the other cards, she loses that round.

Shuffle the index cards and place one card under each piece

of cardboard, remembering which cardboard "door" conceals the card with the smiling face. Prompt your child to point to one of the three doors. If she points to the winning door, remove one of the other doors and the card underneath it, so that two doors remain. If instead she points to a nonwinning door, remove the other nonwinning door and the card underneath it, so that two doors remain.

Prompt your child to point to one of the two remaining doors, and reveal the card hidden underneath it.

Repeat the game multiple times, until you get a sense of whether your child adopts a particular strategy and whether that strategy changes over time. For instance, she might always "stay," selecting the same door from a choice of two as she did from a choice of three. Or she might always switch, selecting from a choice of two whichever door she hadn't selected from a choice of three. Or she might go back and forth between the two strategies.

 THE HYPOTHESIS

Your child is most likely to employ either a consistent switching strategy or a variable strategy that leans more toward switching over time.

THE RESEARCH

Researchers in a 2012 study examined how three distinct populations—pigeons, preschoolers, and college psychology students—responded to the Monty Hall problem over repeated trials. The problem is named after the host of the game show *Let's Make a Deal*, which popularized the concept. Three doors were shown. Behind two doors were worthless prizes, and behind one was a prize of great value. Contestants selected a door, and then one of the doors that did not contain the grand prize was opened. Contestants could then either opt to stay with their original selection or switch to the other unopened door. The odds of winning the prize are better if you switch, but adults often opt not to.

In the 2012 study, preschoolers were given instructions on how to play a game similar to the one described in the experiment here, and their performance was observed over the course of fifty trials. The results showed that only about a quarter of the children adopted a consistent staying strategy, in which they always selected the same door in the second part of the trial as in the first part. The rest of the participants either consistently switched doors or varied their strategy, with an increased preference for switching in later trials. This increased tendency to switch indicates that children have some rudimentary understanding of probability and notice that switching leads to winning more often than staying does.

As a group, the preschoolers' performance across trials was remarkably similar to the college students' performance. In both groups, the average was about 67 percent switching.

That performance was also quite similar to the ending performance of a group of twelve male white Carneau pigeons. Each pigeon was placed in an apparatus containing three small keys that all started out illuminated. After a pigeon pecked one of the three keys, one of the other keys would be darkened, so that only two keys remained illuminated. If the pigeon then pecked the "winning" key, it would be rewarded with some grain. The pigeons started out around chance level in their selections, but eventually ended up switching, rather than staying, about 60 percent of the time.

One of the reasons the college students were compared to preschoolers and pigeons is because the researchers wanted to see if the birds and the kids might perform better than the students. Adults are notoriously bad at the Monty Hall problem. It is thought that one reason why they tend to stay with their original selection is because it helps minimize regret. After all, it's one thing to lose but another thing to lose when the prize was unknowingly within your grasp. The researchers thought the pigeons and preschoolers would not be affected by this regret-minimization factor and would therefore make more optimal choices than the adults. But it appears that the Monty Hall problem is similarly tricky for those groups, although with repeated trials there are opportunities for learning, even among the birds.

THE TAKEAWAY

Probability theory isn't typically part of the preschool curriculum, but the Monty Hall problem illustrates some key points. For parents, it reveals that your child's statistical and decision-making abilities are so sophisticated, even at this young age, that they can rival the performance of college students on this task. For the children themselves, one practical takeaway is that even when you pursue the optimal strategy of switching every time, sometimes you end up selecting the losing door. You might think that in a game in which not much is at stake, a loss should be easy to handle, but your child is still developing emotional regulation and might take the loss hard. This is a good opportunity to emphasize the virtues of being a gracious loser. Remind your child that nobody likes to lose, but when we handle a loss without throwing a fit or bursting into tears, we can more readily begin round two and take another shot at the prize.

Monkeys on Monty

Other animals have also been presented with the Monty Hall problem. In a 2013 study, both human adults and male rhesus monkeys completed multiple trials of the problem. Each species, on average, demonstrated a greater tendency to switch rather than stay as the trials progressed, although in both populations there were some members who flip-flopped between the strategies even as the trials progressed, or stuck with a "stay" strategy throughout the testing. The researchers concluded that in both human and monkey populations, at least some members have the capacity to learn that switching improves one's odds of winning—although they noted that neither species got as close to an optimal strategy as pigeons did in previous research.

38 Shape-shifting Sensitivity

AGE RANGE: 3 to 5 years

RESEARCH AREA: Perception

 THE EXPERIMENT

You are going to play a few rounds of a game in which your child will look at a group of images and find the one that is not the same as the others. Explain to your child that in each round of the game, you will show her a column that contains three images. Two of the images are the same, and one is different. She should point to the one that is different.

The three columns containing the images are located on page 250. Show your child each column and note how long it takes her to identify the nonmatching image.

THE HYPOTHESIS

It will take your child longer to identify the nonmatching image in the second column than in the first and third columns.

THE RESEARCH

Humans have an impressive ability to recognize objects. Children who see a single illustration of an animal from one particular angle are often able to form a mental model of the animal and later recognize examples shown from other perspectives. How does this learning take place? Researchers in a 2014 study, building on prior research that showed adults have a special sensitivity to certain properties of objects, looked at whether preschool-age children are also sensitive to those properties.

If you look at an image of a standard cylinder, the sides are straight and parallel to each other. But it is possible to deform the cylinder so the sides either curve out, forming a bulge in the middle, or curve in like an hourglass. Previous research has shown that adults are more sensitive to the difference between a cylinder with straight sides and one with curved sides than they are to the difference between two cylinders whose sides both curve but to different degrees. Why is this? Well, when we observe an object with a straight edge, we can generally assume that the edge remains straight regardless of our perspective.

There are only a few viewing angles in which that would not be so. The same goes for a curved edge. But as we view objects from different angles, the magnitude of curvature of an edge may indeed change. Thus, researchers think humans pay special attention to "non-accidental" properties, such as whether an edge is straight or curved, because those properties are key indicators of an object's three-dimensional shape.

In the 2014 study, preschoolers were shown a group of three 3-D objects, two of which matched, and were asked to identify the nonmatching object. In some of the trials, the difference between the matching and nonmatching objects was a non-accidental property, such as a straight versus a curved edge. In other trials, the difference was a "metric" property, meaning there was a difference in the value or intensity of the curvature.

The results showed that it took the children longer to identify the nonmatching image when the difference was a metric property than when it was a non-accidental property. The average response time for metric properties was 2.56 seconds, whereas the average response time for non-accidental properties was 1.91 seconds.

The researchers concluded that preschoolers do have a special sensitivity to non-accidental properties, and this sensitivity may help explain why young children can so quickly learn to recognize new objects.

 **THE TAKEAWAY**

By the time your child reaches her preschool years, she is likely already very adept at visual recognition of objects, and the results of this research show that there are some core features of how she perceives objects that help her along. Keep this in mind when you are drawing pictures with your child. Children can recognize drawings even when certain properties, such as length or angles, are distorted, or when three-dimensional cues, such as shading, are absent. But when straight lines are changed to curves and vice versa, or when lines that are supposed to be parallel are not, it can become more difficult for children (and adults) to make out the scene. If you're trying to draw a pumpkin, you can make its shape more or less oblong, but unless you're trying to emulate a Minecraft style, don't make it rectangular.

Working Memory Workout

AGE: 4 years

RESEARCH AREAS: Memory and attention, executive function

THE EXPERIMENT

You're going to conduct a few exercises that help measure your child's ability to memorize.

You'll conduct the first exercise, the Backward Order Task, on one day; the second exercise, the Six Squares Task, on the next day; and the third exercise, a repeat of the Backward Order Task, a couple of days later.

The Backward Order Task requires no supplies. For the Six Squares Task, you'll need to gather six pieces of construction paper, each a different color, and cut each into a four-inch square. You'll also need twenty-four small stickers that can be used as rewards. Each sticker should be small enough to be completely concealed under one of the squares.

In the Backward Order Task, you'll recite the names of familiar objects, then ask your child to recite the names in reverse order. The first time you conduct the exercise, use the following sets of words and note how many sets your child correctly recites backward:

- Table, plant
- Bicycle, candy
- Mouse, cup, window
- Oven, pencil, ball
- Zipper, candle, puppy, rake
- Diaper, noodle, cloud, pepper

In the Six Squares Task, begin by laying out the six squares of construction paper on a table. Place one sticker under each of the six squares. Allow your child to select a square, then take the sticker under it and give it to him as a reward. Now have him turn away while you rearrange the squares, making sure that the stickers stay underneath their associated squares. Now you'll repeat the process. Each time, your child should select a square. If there is a sticker under the square, give it to him as a reward. Continue the game until he has found all the stickers. To do this efficiently, he'll need to keep a mental record of which color squares he has already checked, regardless of their position on the table. Repeat the Six Squares Task three times, and as you progress, try to extend the time you take to reorder the squares, to keep the task challenging.

Finally, a couple of days later, repeat the Backward Order Task with the following sets of words:

- Jelly, bucket

- Leaf, ladder

- Truck, slipper, cheese

- Ice, scissors, yarn

- Phone, star, ketchup, elbow

- Pocket, worm, bracelet, arrow

Again, make a note of how many sets your child correctly recites backward.

 THE HYPOTHESIS

Your child will show improved performance on the Backward Order Task the second time around.

THE RESEARCH

Working memory is like a small mental scratch pad. It can't hold much information, so our minds frequently erase some or all of the notes we've jotted down to make room for more. Still, that scratch pad can come in handy. For instance, you can use it to remember a phone number until you dial it, or to remember how to navigate to a store in the mall after looking up directions.

Researchers in a 2015 study explored whether children's working memory could be strengthened by a short training program. They gave the children a version of the Backward Order Task prior to the training to establish a baseline, and then again after the training to determine whether the children improved on the task.

The children were split into two groups. The experiment group participated in the training program, which consisted of four weekly sessions. During each session, the children spent about twenty minutes on exercises designed to strengthen working memory, including a version of the Six Squares Task. The control group also had four weekly sessions, but children in this group engaged in tasks that did not involve working memory. Children in both groups were then tested a week after the sessions concluded, as well as three months later.

The results showed that children who participated in the training program did significantly better at the Backward Order Task than those in the control group, not only a week after the program concluded but also three months later. The researchers concluded, "This enduring effect in the current study is striking, given the relatively short training program involved."

 THE TAKEAWAY

If short training sessions can have such lasting effects, then it makes sense to try to keep the momentum going, doesn't it? Fortunately, there are quite a few training exercises that you can try with your child to help him flex this part of his brain. One other exercise you might try is called the One-Back Task. During this task, you show your child a series of images, one at a time, and your child must give a signal, such as a thumbs-up, if the image matches the previous image shown. You can vary the difficulty of the task by adjusting the length of time each image is shown and the length of time between images. Keep track of your child's accuracy, and if you notice improvement, that's both a reason to cheer and a potential indicator of a long-lasting developmental gain.

40 Integrated Facts

AGE: 4 years

RESEARCH AREAS: Memory and attention, learning

THE EXPERIMENT

Read the following short story to your child:

> One day, a squirrel sailed out to sea in her sailboat and met a friendly whale.
>
> The whale used squeaks and squawks to say hello, but then it had to leave and look for its group.
>
> The squirrel was sad that the whale had to go, but now she knew that whales use squeaks and squawks to talk.

Next, spend about ten minutes playing with your child. Then, read this story:

The squirrel who met the friendly whale continued sailing all day.

As the sun began to set, the whale appeared again with four other whales.

"Hello again," said the squirrel. "I see you found your group!"

"Yes," said the whale. "This is my pod. Would you like to play with us?"

The squirrel wanted to play, but she had to sail home for the night. She was sad she had to go, but now she knew that a group of whales is called a pod.

Now spend about fifteen minutes doing an activity with your child. Finally, ask her, "How do members of a pod talk to each other?" If she is unable to give the correct answer, offer her the following three choices: (1) with roars and howls, (2) with squeaks and squawks, (3) with oohs and ahs.

About a week later, remind your child that a group of whales is called a pod. Then, ask the same question you posed in the previous session: "How do members of a pod talk to each other?" If she is unable to give the correct answer, offer her the same three options as before.

 ## THE HYPOTHESIS

Your child is unlikely to be able to answer the question prior to being given the multiple-choice answers. But in each session, she'll be more likely than not to answer correctly once given the three options. In fact, it's possible she'll do a better job in the follow-up session than in the first session, during which the stories were read.

 THE RESEARCH

Integration of knowledge acquired at different times is a skill that helps us better understand the world around us. If we learn at one time that whales communicate with squeaks and squawks, and we learn at a later time that a group of whales is called a pod, then by integrating that information we can arrive at the fact that members of a pod communicate with squeaks and squawks.

Researchers in a 2016 study explored the degree to which four-year-olds are able to integrate information acquired in different learning episodes and to retain that information over time. The children were read a short story that conveyed a fact about the natural world. After a period of unrelated activity, they heard a second short story that conveyed another fact about the natural world. The information from each fact could be integrated to derive a new fact. The children were tested about this derived fact fifteen minutes after hearing the second story, then again a week later.

The results showed that only a small number of children were able to give the answer to the test question about the derived fact when they were asked in an open-ended manner. But when the question was posed with three possible choices, more than half of the children identified the correct answer, much more than would be expected by chance. All told, about 60 percent of participants identified the correct answer either by volunteering it or selecting from multiple choices. That total also held true when the children were tested a week later.

In a related experiment, the researchers found that children's performance on the test question improved in the follow-up session when they were given a reminder about one of the two facts necessary to derive the integrated fact. About 75 percent of the children were able to identify the correct answer if they received a reminder immediately before being asked the test question.

Previous research had determined that school-aged children were able to retain integrated facts, and this study showed that children as young as four years old could also do so. It also showed that when children are given reminders of one of the source facts, it improves their ability to recall the integrated fact.

 THE TAKEAWAY

Think about the wide swath of knowledge that would be inaccessible to your child if not for the ability to make inferences. Her brain's ability to take information acquired at different times, stitch it together, and squeeze out extra information from the integrated data is a process that is already developing in the preschool years. This is challenging, and sometimes a child may struggle to identify or recall information obtained through integration. However, the results of this research suggest that sometimes a child needs only a gentle nudge in the right direction, as through reminders of the source facts or a narrow range of options from which to choose. As a parent, if you observe that your child is not immediately able to rattle off an integrated fact, don't jump to the conclusion that she doesn't know it. Instead, you might try to jog her memory by offering hints or reminders, or by suggesting a few possibilities without giving her the answer outright. You may be surprised to find that the information is already on the tip of her tongue.

41 The Playground Judge

AGE RANGE: 4 to 5 years

RESEARCH AREAS: Social development, morality

 THE EXPERIMENT

For this project, you'll show your child the four scenes depicted in the illustrations on page 251, which center on two types of moral transgressions he is likely to be familiar with: hitting and teasing.

Show your child the first scene, which shows Kid A hitting Kid B, and ask him the following questions:

- Is it OK or not OK for the child to hit? Why or why not?

- If it's not OK, is it a little bit bad or very bad? Why?

- Should the child get in trouble for hitting? Why or why not?

- If the child should get in trouble, a little bit of trouble or a lot? Why?

- How do you think Kid A feels? How do you think Kid B feels?

Now show your child the second scene, which shows Kid B hitting Kid A in retaliation. Explain that after Kid B was hit, he decided to hit back. Ask the same set of questions about this second scene.

For the third and fourth scenes, which depict unprovoked teasing (in which one child sticks their tongue out at the other) and retaliatory teasing, respectively, follow the same procedure and ask the same set of questions as they pertain to teasing.

 ## THE HYPOTHESIS

Your child is likely to judge both the provoked and unprovoked actions as morally wrong and deserving of punishment, but he may not be able to fully explain why, and he may judge the unprovoked actions as more serious offenses than the retaliatory actions.

 ## THE RESEARCH

Children in kindergarten through fourth grade participated in a 2003 study in which they were presented with the hitting and teasing scenarios and then interviewed about them. The study's authors were interested in how children form moral judgments and attribute emotions to other people.

They found that younger children are more likely to view the retaliatory actions as less serious than the unprovoked actions, although still morally wrong. Older children, in contrast, tend to judge both the unprovoked and retaliatory actions as seriously wrong, which suggests that they understand the acts to be morally wrong in an objective sense. Younger children overwhelmingly described the victims of the actions as sad, whereas in older children a greater percentage attributed both sadness and anger to the victims.

 **THE TAKEAWAY**

You've probably noticed that your child is able to pick up on certain basic moral principles, such as "hitting is wrong," at an early age. But it takes time for him to fully understand why it's wrong and to be able to explain it clearly. You can help your child develop a more robust understanding of moral rules by explaining the "why" behind the rule. You might point out, for instance, the ways in which hitting or teasing harm the victim. You might also point out that in many cases, the person who hits or teases also suffers negative consequences because of his or her behavior. Being able to clearly understand the "why" behind moral choices is an important step in the process by which your child learns to internalize (and hopefully live out) moral behavior.

42 The "Knew It All Along" Error

AGE RANGE: 4 to 5 years

RESEARCH AREAS: Memory and attention, metacognition

 THE EXPERIMENT

On the opposite page are four panels, each of which contains a drawing of an animal and a fact related to the animal. Each of the facts includes a word in italics that is likely to be unfamiliar to your child, which helps ensure that the facts are novel and not something your child already knows about the animal. In the top two panels, the facts are generalized and apply to all animals of a given type. In the bottom two panels, the facts are specific and apply to the individual animal shown in the picture.

In whichever order you like, show your child each of the panels. Read the panel's fact to your child twice while pointing to the

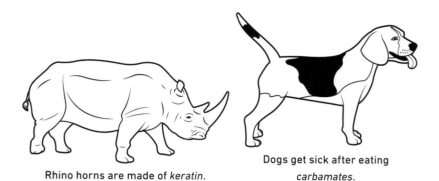

Rhino horns are made of *keratin*.

Dogs get sick after eating *carbamates*.

This bird feeds her babies *regurgitated* food.

This seal sleeps on its *dorsal* side.

animal in the drawing. After reading the fact, say something like, "Huh!" or "That's interesting!" to indicate that you were previously unaware of the fact. Then, for each panel, ask your child about when she came to learn the fact you presented. For instance, in the first panel, you might say, "Did you know about this before we read it just now? Did you know that rhino horns are made of keratin?"

THE HYPOTHESIS

It is more likely for the top panels than for the bottom panels that your child will indicate she has always known the fact presented, or at least had known the fact before you read it to her.

THE RESEARCH

A 2012 study had found that children in preschool and early grade school demonstrated better recall of statements that applied to a category of things (such as "Boys like a vegetable called fep") than statements that applied to individual persons or things (such as "He likes a vegetable called fep"), suggesting that children have a predisposition toward learning about kinds and categories.

Researchers in a 2015 study wanted to explore whether this predisposition would hold true for a particular error that people of all ages, but especially children, tend to make when learning new facts: After learning the fact, they have trouble recalling what they used to think before they learned it. It's thought that the brain gives preference to the newly acquired information, making one's former understanding more difficult to access. In some cases, this inability to distinguish between the new and old leads a person to erroneously believe that they have always known the new information, or at least that they knew it before they actually learned it.

In the 2015 study, preschoolers and slightly older children sat with an experimenter and looked through a book that presented panels similar to those in this project. Some of the panels presented generalized facts, which applied to an entire species of animal, and some presented individualized facts, which applied to the specific animal pictured. For each fact, the child was asked whether he or she had known the fact all along.

The researchers found that "I knew it all along" assertions were common among the four- and five-year-olds in the study, but there was a difference between their responses for generalized and individualized facts. On average, about 57 percent of four- and five-year-olds thought they had known the generalized facts all along, whereas only 47 percent thought they had known the individualized facts all along. (Slightly older children were less likely to make "I knew it all along" assertions, but the difference in response rates between generalized and individualized facts remained.)

The results of the study support the theory that kind-based facts are especially easy for children to acquire and process, and because they become integrated so seamlessly, the difference between new and old information is particularly difficult to distinguish, leading to more "knew it all along" errors.

 **THE TAKEAWAY**

For parents and preschool educators, being aware that children acquire category-based information especially easily can help shape how children are taught. In cases in which categorical statements are accurate and appropriate, such as "Cold-blooded animals become hotter or cooler depending on the temperature of their surroundings," it might be helpful to impart these facts using the categorical statement, rather than talking about any individual cold-blooded animal, such as a pet reptile. But it's equally important to know that children's predisposition toward category-based information can have a downside. For instance, if they hear a negative stereotype, which is a categorical statement about a group of people, the child's ability to absorb it so easily— even to the point that she thinks she's always known it—might make the stereotype hard to dispel. Because of this, try to prevent those stereotypes from being planted in her mind in the first place, and if they do start to sprout, try to address the problem early, before they have time to form deep roots.

43 Bended Estimates

AGE RANGE: 4 to 5 years

RESEARCH AREA: Number sense

 THE EXPERIMENT

On a sheet of paper, draw a ten-inch-long line. Place hatch marks on either end, and label them with the numbers 1 and 10. Next, on a separate piece of paper, draw another line of the same length and place hatch marks on the ends. Label one hatch mark with the number 1 and the other with the number 100.

Provide your child with a pencil and the sheet with the 1 and 10 labels. Explain that the line on the paper is a number line that begins with 1 and ends with 10. Tell him that you are going to say some numbers between 1 and 10, and he should draw a dot on the number line where he thinks the number belongs. Say the following numbers: 6, 3, 9, 4, 2, 8, 7.

Next, present the sheet with the 1 and 100 labels. Explain

that the line on the paper is a number line that begins with 1 and ends with 100. Tell your child you are going to say some numbers between 1 and 100, and he should do the same thing as with the other number line: draw a dot where he thinks the number belongs. Say the following numbers: 25, 3, 86, 4, 6, 18, 71, 2, 48, 67.

After your child completes the exercise, get out your ruler and place hatch marks at the correct positions for the numbers your child was asked to identify.

 THE HYPOTHESIS

On the 1–10 number line, your child's estimates are likely to be relatively accurate and have a linear fit, in which the numbers under 5 tend to be on the left and the numbers over 5 tend to be on the right. But for the 1–100 number line, your child's estimates are likely to be much less accurate and have more of a logarithmic fit, in which the numbers under 20 tend to be on the left and the numbers above 20 tend to be on the right.

 THE RESEARCH

Children in a 2010 study were presented with two number-line tasks similar to those in this project. The researchers examined the accuracy of the children's estimates, and they also looked at whether the children conceptualized the number line as having either a linear scale (in which each integer is an equal distance away from the next) or a logarithmic scale (in which larger numbers have less distance between them than smaller numbers do).

For the 1–10 number line, the results showed that younger preschoolers tended to produce estimates that fit a logarithmic scale, while children a year or two older tended to produce estimates that fit a linear scale. But for the 1–100 number line, children in all age groups tested, up to six years old, tended to produce logarithmic estimates.

One simple explanation for why children exhibit this tendency toward logarithmic estimates is that they are more familiar with the smaller numbers than with the larger numbers in the studied range. But that explanation has been found inadequate. For instance, in a 2003 study, fourth graders were found to use a logarithmic strategy when estimating numbers' position on a 0 to 1,000 scale, even though by fourth grade they were already very familiar with numbers up to a thousand.

So if children's degree of familiarity with the numbers doesn't completely explain the phenomenon, what does? Well, these results were consistent with a theory presented in a 2004 study that children's number sense actually relies on two distinct systems: one that is able to accurately recognize small quantities, and another that is used to approximate larger quantities on a logarithmic number line. As children grow older, that mental number line tends to become more linear—but it may be the case that the logarithmic number sense isn't replaced, but rather augmented. In other words, older children and adults might keep their logarithmic number sense but additionally acquire the ability to map numbers onto a linear number line, and then come to better understand when linear estimation is appropriate.

🔍 THE TAKEAWAY

Learning how to accurately estimate the position of values that fall in a given range is a foundational skill that enables us to do all sorts of everyday things. For instance, folding a letter to fit in a standard-size envelope and drawing a tic-tac-toe board both require you to understand, at least in a rudimentary way, that the distance between one-third and two-thirds is the same as the distance between zero and one-third, and between two-thirds and one.

As your child develops his number sense, keep in mind that just because he knows the name for a number, or can recognize its shape, or can count that number of things in a group, it doesn't mean that he fully understands the relationship between that number and other numbers. (In fact, most of us adults still have a thing or two to learn.)

Although not every child will end up being a math professor, you can still do some simple things to encourage numerical literacy. Play counting games. Let your child be your assistant when you are using measuring tools, such as scales, measuring cups, or rulers. Pose simple "greater than" and "less than" problems. Above all, treat math not as a chore but as an adventure.

Absorption Awareness

AGE RANGE: 4 to 5 years

RESEARCH AREAS: Memory and attention, judgment

THE EXPERIMENT

Photocopy and cut out the eight pictures of animals that accompany this project on the opposite page. Explain to your child that you are going to introduce her to some animal friends, and that she should try to remember their names. Present each animal to your child in any order you wish. For the four animals whose names are associated with the animal in some way, introduce the animal by saying its name, and also note the association. For instance, you might say, "This animal's name is Oinky, because pigs say oink," or "This animal's name is Hoppy, because frogs like to hop." For the four animals whose names are not associated

Oinky

Hoppy

Clucky

Buzzy

Jane

Miguel

Jeremiah

Larisa

with the animal, you can just introduce the animal by name without explaining how it got its name. For instance, "This animal's name is Jane."

After you have introduced the name of each animal, present each picture again and ask your child to recall its name. Note whether your child is able to accurately recall the animal's name. Then ask your child, "Do you think you will remember this animal's name if I ask you about it later today?" Note your child's response.

Next, pair up the pictures so that each pair consists of an animal with an associated name and an animal with a name that has no association. Present each pair to your child and ask her which of the two animals' names she thinks she is more likely to remember later. Note her selection for each of the four pairs.

Move on to an unrelated activity, such as coloring a page in a coloring book, for about two minutes. Then present each of the eight animal pictures and ask your child to recall its name. Note whether she is able to accurately do so.

 THE HYPOTHESIS

The first time you ask your child to name the animals she was just shown, she is likely to express overconfidence that she will remember their names later on. In fact, she might even indicate that she will be able to recall the names later even if she failed to remember them on the spot. When you present pairs of images, though, she will accurately predict which of the images she is more likely to recall later, as measured by how many of the four chosen images she is able to recall, versus the four images that were unchosen.

 THE RESEARCH

A 2013 study tested preschoolers' ability to make accurate judgments about their own learning. In one experiment, the children were taught the names of stuffed animals. Half of the animals had names that were associated with the animal in some way, and the other half did not. After teaching a child the names, the experimenter presented each stuffed animal, asked the child to recall its name, and then asked the child whether they thought they would recall the animal's name at a later time. Then, after a delay, the child was quizzed about the stuffed animals' names.

The results showed that young children tend to be strongly overconfident in their recall abilities. On average, they indicated that they expected to be able to recall the animal's name about 87 percent of the time, but when they were later quizzed, they were able to recall the names only about 47 percent of the time. Moreover, about half of the children expressed total confidence in their recall abilities, meaning they expected to be able to remember the names of every stuffed animal they were taught. And even when children failed to immediately recall a name prior to making their predictions, some still indicated that they expected to be able to recall the name at a later time.

The researchers suspected that the children were exhibiting a yes bias—meaning they tended to respond yes reflexively. To try to eliminate this yes bias, researchers ran a follow-up experiment in which the children were presented with pairs of animals and asked to indicate which animal's name they were more likely to recall at a later time. This type of question, they thought, would work around the yes bias by requiring the children to compare two possibilities and select the one they felt stronger confidence about.

The results showed that the children still exhibited overconfidence in their recall abilities, but when they were presented with a pair of animals, one with a name they were able to immediately recall and another with a name they could not recall, the children almost always chose the former over the latter as the animal whose name they expected to be able to recall later. This suggests that young children do, in fact, understand that if they fail to recall a name immediately, they will likely struggle to remember it later on as well.

THE TAKEAWAY

Oh, to have a preschooler's confidence. They are highly skilled athletes, impeccable dancers, extraordinary singers, and possessors of ultimate bravery, genius-level smarts, and unparalleled humility. The results of this research suggest that we can add "photographic memory" to their long list of special skills. Yet even though the reality of their memorization abilities tends to fall far short of what they envision, studies such as this one reveal that even young children are able to make judgments about the inner workings of their own minds, which is no small feat.

One way to help your child become better attuned to her own limitations and make more accurate judgments of learning is to help her avoid a mere impulsive response. You might gently point out that although our brains are really amazing, memorizing information can be hard, and that people have lapses in memory all the time. You might even remind her of a past instance when she's struggled to recall a person's name, as a way of helping her realize that realistically, she's not always going to retain 100 percent of what she takes in. Take care not to present these reminders as criticism, though. The intent is to help her think more clearly, not to knock her down a peg. And even if she persists in her overconfident self-assessments, remember that being at least a little overconfident can help children summon the courage to take risks and try new things, which is important for their development.

Judgment Helps

Asking study participants to make judgments about their own learning can help researchers better comprehend how well the subjects understand their own abilities to remember content. Recent research has demonstrated that making judgments of learning can also have an effect on the participants' performance. For instance, a 2015 study presented participants with pairs of words that were either related or unrelated. One group of participants made a judgment of learning, indicating how likely they thought they would be to remember the words later, and another group did not. Later, both groups were tested on their recall abilities. Both groups remembered more related pairs than unrelated pairs, but the group that had made judgments of learning performed better than the other group in recalling the related pairs.

Building on these results, a 2018 study investigated whether judgments of learning help people remember related pairs of words, negatively affect their memory of unrelated pairs, or both. Across a series of experiments, researchers found that judgments of learning help memory more than they hurt it.

These findings suggest that one way to help students remember the material they are studying is to ask them to make judgments about their ability to retain it.

The Batman Effect

 THE EXPERIMENT

You will need an age-appropriate academic workbook or work-sheets that would take your child at least twenty minutes to complete. You will also need an attractive age-appropriate game that can be played by your child on a phone, tablet, or handheld device.

Present the workbook to your child and explain that it is an important activity, and that it would be helpful for him to work as hard as he can on it for the next eight minutes. Tell him that he might occasionally want to take a break from the activity and play the video game, and that he may choose to take a break at any time. Explain that you will be busy working on a project of your own during this time, but you will remind him every two minutes about working hard on the workbook. During the eight minutes, use a stopwatch or timer to track how much of the time he spends on the workbook. Every two minutes, deliver a reminder message: "Am I working hard?"

Sometime later, you will repeat the same activity, but this time, encourage him to pretend that he is a character who is known for working hard, such as Batman or Dora the Explorer. If you have any dress-up clothes or accessories related to the character, allow your child to wear them. Tell him that it would be helpful for his character to work as hard as he can on the workbook, but that he can take breaks and play the video game if he wishes. Again, track how much of the time he spends on the workbook. Every two minutes, deliver a reminder message that incorporates his character's name. For instance, if he is pretending to be Batman, the reminder message might be "Is Batman working hard?"

 THE HYPOTHESIS

Your child will spend more time on the workbook when pretending to be a character who is known to be hardworking.

THE RESEARCH

Children in a 2017 study were assigned an intentionally boring, repetitive task, and they were told that they could take breaks whenever they wanted to play a video game. The participants were sorted into several groups. In one group, called the "self-immersed" condition, children were reminded about their task with the question "Am I working hard?" In another group, called the "exemplar" condition, participants were encouraged to pretend that they were a character known for working hard, such as Batman, and were reminded about their task with a question pertaining to their character, such as "Is Batman working hard?" The researchers found that across conditions, most children spent more time on the game than they did on the task they had been asked to work on. Four-year-olds spent more time on the video game than six-year-olds, suggesting that children develop a greater sense of perseverance during this point in their growth.

Experimenters also found that the children who were in the "self-immersed" condition spent more time playing the video game than the children in the "exemplar" condition. The researchers think that when children take on the perspective of another person, particularly a familiar character who has positive traits, such as power, diligence, and a good work ethic, they are better able to disengage from a self-centered perspective that tends to be more focused on immediate gratification.

🔍 THE TAKEAWAY

Your child is a highly distractible creature. Shiny things, bouncy things, things on a screen, and things that make fart noises will cause him to veer off task, but you can combat these distractions, at least to a small degree, by encouraging him to assume the mantle of a hardworking superhero, storybook character, or other persevering protagonist. More generally, when your child engages in dress-up and role-play, he may be trying on not only a character's outfit but also that character's perspective and personality. In addition to helping him improve his work ethic, it may help him see a situation through a new lens or become more comfortable exhibiting positive traits such as bravery and integrity.

46 Know Your Audience

AGE RANGE: 4 to 5 years

RESEARCH AREAS: Social development, communication

 THE EXPERIMENT

Select one of the two illustrations that accompany this project, and introduce a stuffed animal or puppet to your child. For instance, you might select the picture of the guitar. Explain that in the place where the puppet lives, there are no guitars, and the puppet doesn't know anything about them. Then, show your child the picture of the guitar and say, "Here's a guitar. Can you tell the puppet about it?" Allow your child to describe the guitar, and take note of her responses. In particular, pay attention to whether she describes general information about guitars (such as "You use them to play music") or specific information about

the particular guitar in the picture (such as "It has six strings" or "It is resting on a stand").

Next, explain that in the place where the puppet lives, there are many dogs, and the puppet knows a *lot* about dogs. Then, show your child the picture of the dog and say, "Here's a dog. Can you tell the puppet about it?" Again, allow your child to describe the dog, and pay attention to whether her responses describe general or specific information.

 THE HYPOTHESIS

At four years old, your child is likely to offer the same amount of general information in each case, but she is likely to tailor the amount of specific information based on whether the puppet is described as knowledgeable or ignorant about the object. She'll offer more specific information when the puppet is knowledgeable and less when the puppet is ignorant.

At five years old, however, your child is likely to tailor both the general and the specific information to her audience, focusing more on general properties when the puppet is described as ignorant and more on specific details when the puppet is described as well informed.

 THE RESEARCH

In a 2018 study, four- and five-year-olds were shown images of common objects and asked to describe the objects to a stuffed bear who was characterized as either ignorant about or familiar with the object. The researchers then coded the children's responses according to whether they described general information that would apply to any object in the same category or specific information about the object that distinguishes it from other objects in the same category. An analysis found that the four-year-old participants' descriptions did not appear to take into account the stuffed bear's knowledge or lack thereof about the object when offering general information. They offered roughly the same amount of general information regardless of what they were told about the bear's familiarity with the object. However, they did appear to take into account the stuffed bear's knowledge when offering specific information. Five-year-olds, on the other hand, adjusted both the amount of general information and the amount of specific information based on the stuffed bear's familiarity with the object.

The researchers concluded that by four years old, children are already beginning to take into account a person's existing knowledge to craft relevant communication, and by five years old, they have further developed this skill.

 THE TAKEAWAY

Younger preschoolers tend to state the obvious, recounting events to you even though you were with them at the time, or "teaching" you a concept that you taught *them* only moments before. It might be tempting to try to cut them short, but informational communication is a skill that is refined through practice, so when possible, allow your child to tell you about things that interest her, even if you're already very familiar with them. With time, she will come to better understand what you already know or don't know. And with some gentle hints, she'll eventually figure out that when communicating with another person, there's no need to inform them about things they already know. Until she masters these unspoken rules, exercise patience and try to enjoy her lectures and lessons. You might not learn anything new from her, but with the right mind-set you can come to appreciate her best efforts.

⟨47⟩ Fantastic Work

AGE RANGE: 4 to 5 years

RESEARCH AREAS: Cognitive development, pretend play, executive function

 THE EXPERIMENT

Photocopy and cut out the illustrations of animals on pages 252–253. Some of the illustrations have heads and bodies that match, and others do not. Explain to your child that you will show him the illustrations one at a time, and his job is to say the name of the animal body depicted. If the head does not match the body, he should ignore the head and only say the name of the animal's body. As you go through each of the pictures, make note of how many errors your child makes on the illustrations with mismatched bodies, and also note whether the difference in

222

reaction time is minimal or noticeable, depending on whether the head and body are mismatched.

Now calculate your child's fantasy scores by answering the following questions:

1) Does your child have an imaginary friend? (Yes/No)

2) On a scale from 1 (very low) to 10 (very high), how would you rate your child's interest and belief in fantastical entities, such as Santa Claus, the Tooth Fairy, monsters, leprechauns, and so on?

3) On a scale from 1 (very low) to 10 (very high), how would you describe your child's preference for toys and games that involve fantasy and make-believe?

 THE HYPOTHESIS

If your child performs well on the animal illustrations task—making few errors and having essentially the same response time for the matching and mismatched animals—he is more likely to have an imaginary friend, a higher score for question 2, and a lower score for question 3. If your child struggles with the animal illustrations task, he is less likely to have an imaginary friend, and his score for question 2 is likely to be low, while his score for question 3 is likely to be high.

THE RESEARCH

A 2013 study looked at how inhibitory control, which is a child's ability to prevent an automatic or impulsive action and instead substitute a different action, is correlated with the degree to which the child is oriented toward fantasy. One of the measures of inhibitory control used in the study was a task similar to the one you did with the animal illustrations. Children were shown images of animals with either matching or mismatched heads and bodies and were instructed to name the animals' bodies. The experimenters measured the number of errors the children made, along with the amount of time it took the participants to say an animal name after being shown the pictures.

The children's parents and teachers also completed a questionnaire related to the children's interest in fantasy, and the children were also interviewed about the same topic. The researchers then looked at how that data was associated with the children's performance on the inhibitory control test. They found that children who had imaginary friends or who held beliefs about fantastical creatures had more uniform response times. In contrast, children without these attributes had more of a difference in their response times, depending on whether the animals' bodies matched. A smaller difference in response times between matching and mismatched animals indicates that children with these fantastic inclinations had better-developed inhibitory control skills and were better able to ignore the irrelevant heads and focus only on the animal bodies. Interestingly, the researchers also found that the more errors children made during the test, the more likely they were to have an interest in toys and games that had fantasy or make-believe elements.

Why would one indicator of fantasy orientation be associated with better inhibitory control and another indicator be associated with worse? The study suggests that fantasy that is more cognitively oriented and involves thinking and belief may be related to cognitive flexibility, which in turns helps children inhibit knee-jerk responses. Fantasy that is more behaviorally oriented, such as pretend play with fantastical elements, does not, however, seem to have as much to do with cognitive flexibility.

THE TAKEAWAY

One of the goals of the 2014 study was to determine whether there were developmental benefits to having an orientation toward fantasy, and whether there are distinct components that make up a fantasy interest. The answer is yes on both accounts. For parents, one takeaway is that not all fantasy-oriented children are the same. Some kids may enjoy pretending to be other people or creatures. Others may have conversations with imaginary friends. Still others may enjoy games and toys that introduce them to fantasy worlds. So if you see your child exhibiting some fantasy-oriented behaviors or interests, keep in mind that he might not be inclined toward others. The best way to tell what components of fantasy strike a chord with your child is to give him plenty of opportunities to let his imagination run wild.

Fantasy Camp

The results of the preceding study on fantasy orientation show that there is an association between preschoolers' orientation toward fantasy and their executive function skills, such as inhibitory control. But do better-developed executive function skills cause a greater interest in fantasy, or does exposure to fantasy help improve executive function?

A 2016 study attempted to sort out the causal relationship. Children ages three to five were split into several groups. One group participated in fantasy camp sessions over a five-week period, during which they were encouraged to create a fantastic script and act it out. Another group engaged in non-fantasy-oriented games and activities during the same period, and a third group served as a control and followed their normal routine. For all children, measures of executive function were taken before and after the five-week period. The results revealed that only children in the fantasy camp condition demonstrated an improvement in their executive function skills.

Among children who attended the fantasy camp, one differentiator was the degree to which their pretend play was fantastic in nature. Kids who pretended to be fairies or dragons or other fantastic creatures showed more improvement in their executive function skills than kids whose pretend play was more realistic, such as pretending to be a grown-up visiting a fancy restaurant. Both types of pretend play involve using the imagination, but there seems to be something special about fantasy play that really sharpens the mind.

48 Trying to Forget

AGE RANGE: 4 to 5 years

RESEARCH AREA: Memory and attention

THE EXPERIMENT

Collect an assortment of twelve small household objects that your child easily recognizes. Split them into two sets of six and place each set into a box or other container. Present the first set to your child and explain that his task is to remember all the objects in the box. Allow him to look at and examine the objects.

After about a minute, explain to your child that you gave him the wrong objects to memorize and produce the second box of objects. Direct him to empty his brain so that he can make room for the correct set of objects. Then, show him the second box and allow him to look at and examine those objects.

After another minute has elapsed, put both boxes away and have a brief conversation with your child about what he would like to eat for his next meal. Then, ask him to recall as many objects as he can from the second set, and note how many he is able to remember. Finally, ask him if he can recall any objects from the first set, and again note how many he identifies.

 THE HYPOTHESIS

Your child will recall significantly more objects from the second set than from the first set.

 THE RESEARCH

We often think of forgetting as a defect of memory rather than an active process, but according to the philosopher Friedrich Nietzsche, "Without forgetting it is quite impossible to live at all." Nietzsche saw forgetting as something that could be achieved as an act of will, and an ability we should be grateful we have, because constant rumination on our memories puts us into a state of paralysis. Being able to intentionally forget allows us to filter out irrelevant information so we can better focus on what is pertinent and useful.

It turns out that there are several ways to encourage our brains to forget. Researchers who study directed forgetting have found that adults who are instructed to forget a list of items show poorer recall of those items than adults who are told to remember them. A 2018 study attempted to identify whether the same holds true for young children.

The children were shown a container with several items inside and were instructed to remember them. Then, half of the children were told that they should forget the first set and concentrate on memorizing a second set of items. The other half were told that they should try to remember the items from both sets. After a brief distraction task, the children were asked to recall the objects from both sets. The results showed that children who had been directed to forget were able to recall fewer items from the first set and more items from the second set than children who had been directed to remember both sets of objects.

 **THE TAKEAWAY**

Children with strong recall abilities are often praised, but it may be that determining which information to forget is just as important as knowing what to remember. Fortunately, the results of this research suggest that preschoolers can be given cues to forget unimportant information, and that doing so can help them better remember what's important. You can use the "empty your brain" prompt to facilitate this process. For instance, if you're teaching your child how to play a game, and you realize that you accidentally misspoke about one of the rules, instruct him to clear the old, incorrect rule out of his mind to make room for the new, correct rule. This technique is likely to be useful for small, inconsequential memories, but if your child experiences any sort of serious trauma and is troubled by the memories of the event, don't take a DIY approach. Seek help from a professional who can help him process, cope, and heal.

49 No Sway

AGE RANGE: 5 years

RESEARCH AREAS: Social development, prejudices, probability

THE EXPERIMENT

Explain to your five-year-old that you are going to tell her three short stories, and after each one you'll ask her a few questions.

STORY 1

A store sells both tall candles and short candles. In one week, four tall candles and twenty short candles are sold. Carl is one of the customers who purchased a candle during that time. Carl's candle smells like apples and cinnamon.

- Do you think Carl bought a tall candle or a short candle?

- Why do you think so?

- Were there more tall candles or short candles sold?

STORY 2

Becky is a pretty, outgoing girl who is very popular at school. She sometimes, however, thinks she is better than the other girls. She is in a class with fifteen other girls. Each girl is going to try out for either the cheerleading squad or the marching band. A few of the girls try out to be cheerleaders, but most of them try out for the band.

QUESTION SET 2

- Do you think Becky will try out for the cheerleading squad or the marching band?

- Why do you think so?

- For which activity do most of the girls in the class try out?

STORY 3

At a doctor's office, there are ten patients. Each patient is a mommy or a daddy. The doctor asks each patient what they will do when they go home. Two of them say that they will do the laundry, but eight of them say that they will mow their lawn. A mommy whose name is Mrs. Price is one of the patients.

QUESTION SET 3

- Do you think Mrs. Price will do the laundry or mow the lawn when she gets home?
- Why do you think so?
- Which activity did most of the patients say they will do when they get home?

 ## THE HYPOTHESIS

For the first and second stories, your child is likely to be primarily influenced by probability. She is likely to say that Carl bought a short candle and Becky will try out for the marching band. The more clearly she indicates that she understands the uneven probabilities through her answers to the other questions, the more likely she is to guess the most probable option.

For the third story, however, your child is likely to say that Mrs. Price will do laundry when she gets home, particularly if she has been taught or has been exposed to gender biases related to chores and home maintenance.

 **THE RESEARCH**

Biases and prejudices can sometimes cloud the reasoning of older children and adults, even to the point of making objectively improbable events seem probable.

The authors of a 2011 study wanted to examine the degree to which young children's reasoning might be similarly influenced by stereotypes. They also wanted to identify whether a lack of exposure to a certain stereotype might help young children reason better than older children.

They presented five-year-olds and third graders with scenarios in which the children might make inferences about a person's behavior or preferences based on probability that conflict with inferences based on stereotypes. The researchers employed some stereotypes that tend to be known to both five-year-olds and third graders and some that tend to be known only to the older group. They anticipated that if the younger children were unfamiliar with a certain stereotype, then they couldn't be influenced by it, and they would therefore rely more heavily on probability than the older group would.

The first story you read to your child presents a scenario where no common stereotypes give a clue as to whether Carl is likely to prefer tall candles or short candles. In the absence of such information, the only relevant clue is the fact that there were significantly more short candles sold than tall candles.

Assuming your child is able to identify this fact, she is likely to rely on it and guess that Carl purchased a short candle.

The second story involves a scenario in which a bias might influence older children and adults. But your five-year-old is unlikely to be familiar with the stereotype of cheerleaders being pretty, popular, and vain. Thus, to determine whether Becky is among those who try out for the cheerleading squad or the marching band, your child is likely to consider only the fact that most girls try out for the band.

On the other hand, your five-year-old *is* likely to be familiar with stereotypes around gender roles, and that bias might influence her thinking when presented with the third scenario. With complete ignorance of gender stereotypes, your child would probably say that Mrs. Price will mow the lawn, on the basis that most of the patients intend to do so. But if your child has a notion that laundry is a job that women do and mowing the lawn is a job that men do, then that bias may win out over the choice influenced by probability alone.

Consistent with their hypothesis, the researchers found that five-year-olds were, overall, significantly less likely than the third graders to offer stereotype justifications for their choices and more likely to offer justifications related to probabilities.

THE TAKEAWAY

Keep in mind that biases and stereotypes among young children often arise out of ignorance and overgeneralization. For instance, a child may assume that mowing the lawn is a man's job simply on the basis that her own father mows the lawn at their house.

In contrast, stereotypes that persist among adults tend to be more prejudicial and involve unfair assumptions about a person based on their membership in a category or class.

Although it's practically impossible not to be influenced by any bias whatsoever, being able to recognize bias is the first step in preventing it from improperly influencing our reasoning or decision making. So if you notice your child drawing conclusions or stating opinions that seem to be founded on stereotypes, it may be beneficial to have a conversation about those stereotypes: Where did they come from? How accurate are they? Do they really apply to all members of a category, or is there wide variation among individuals? Is relying on such stereotypes likely to be hurtful to other people? Is it likely to cause us to make foolish decisions?

Closely examining these biases can help you identify and stop some of your own prejudicial thinking and can help prevent it from taking root in your child.

50 A Light Wait

AGE: 5 years

RESEARCH AREAS: Memory and attention, learning

THE EXPERIMENT

You will need two research subjects for this experiment, so pair your child with a friend or sibling the same age or up to two years older. You'll also need another parent or adult friend to act as a helper. Finally, you'll need to select two small paper crafts that you can teach the children how to construct, such as a frog and a crane.

Set up a room so that there is an instructional area in one part, where the crafts can be assembled, and a waiting area that is separate but not far away, with a chair or other spot where a child can sit. The chair should be positioned so that it is facing perpendicular to the instructional area, so someone sitting in the chair would have to turn his or her head to view the instructional area.

Bring both children into the room and explain that you are going to teach each of them how to build a craft. Explain that your helper is there to watch how you teach the crafts. Tell your child that the other child will get the first turn, and then she will get the next turn. Direct her to sit in the waiting area until it's her turn. Direct the other child to sit with you in the instructional area, and teach him how to complete the craft.

Although the helper is ostensibly there to observe your instruction, his or her true purpose is to observe your child in the waiting area. How does she occupy her time while waiting for her turn? How closely does she pay attention to what is going on in the instructional area? Does she pay sustained, close attention? Does she occasionally glance with interest? Does she appear not to be interested at all? Does she display disruptive or attention-seeking behavior? Does she stare off into space, or otherwise ignore the instructional area while waiting for her turn?

Once the first craft is completed, have the children switch places, and repeat the procedure, this time with the other craft.

Sometime later, either at a different time of day or after a few days have passed, offer your child and her sibling or friend (if available) the opportunity to each make the same type of craft that the other completed earlier, but instead of walking each child through it, encourage them to try to complete their crafts on their own. If they request help, start with small hints and move on to bigger hints if needed, but for the most part try to play a hands-off role, and observe how well each is able to complete his or her craft.

THE HYPOTHESIS

During the time your child is sitting in the waiting area, she may have periods of sustained attention, but the majority of the time she will not direct her attention to the instructional area. And, as you might expect, the more closely she pays attention while sitting in the waiting area, the less help she is likely to need when building that craft later on.

THE RESEARCH

A 2009 study recruited pairs of siblings from different cultural backgrounds. Some of the sibling pairs were from middle-class European-American families, and some were from working-class Guatemalan families with limited school experience and relatively low exposure to Western culture.

In each experiment, the younger sibling was observed while waiting for the older sibling to finish putting together a craft. A few days later, the younger child was given an opportunity to assemble the craft that his or her older sibling had worked on, and the experimenters observed the level of adult assistance required to complete the project.

The researchers found a remarkable difference between the European-American children and the Guatemalan children. The European-American children engaged in sustained attention toward their sibling's craft project less than a third of the time they were waiting, whereas the Guatemalan children engaged in sustained attention nearly two-thirds of the time. Also, more than a quarter of the European-American kids were observed exhibiting disruptive or attention-seeking behavior, whereas only a single Guatemalan child out of the forty who participated exhibited such behavior.

When it came time to assemble the craft on their own, children who had engaged in more sustained attention during the earlier session required less adult assistance. Because the Guatemalan children had, on average, paid more attention during the earlier session, they tended to be able to complete the craft with less help than the European-American children.

What accounts for these cultural differences? The researchers think it has to do with differences in learning and teaching styles. In indigenous Central American communities, it is common for children to participate in a range of household and community activities and to learn by keenly watching adults. Learning is driven primarily by observation, rather than by active instruction, and children in these families spend more time doing chores and other productive work than their European-American counterparts. In contrast, for many children in middle-class European-American families, their learning is typically managed by adults, who direct their attention and engage in active instruction. The researchers suggest that this may lead them to become reliant on adults for that direction and to be less capable than their Guatemalan counterparts of directing their attention on their own.

 **THE TAKEAWAY**

Attention and learning generally go hand in hand, which is why it can be such a struggle for children with attention deficit disorders to learn in a traditional school environment. Yet even if a child has the ability to sustain attention, if she doesn't know where and when to direct that attention, she becomes like a satellite receiver that isn't tuned in. The results of this research suggest that giving children ample opportunities to discover on their own where their attention should be directed, rather than simply expecting them to follow instructions, can help them develop this valuable skill. As your child prepares to enter kindergarten, seek out learning environments that encourage self-directed learning, and remember that while scheduled, organized activities have their place, your child can also benefit from unstructured time and from merely being around adults engaging in productive work. You might hear some complaints about boredom from a child unaccustomed to having to direct her own attention, but in the long run she is likely to benefit. And she might even learn how to do a few new chores.

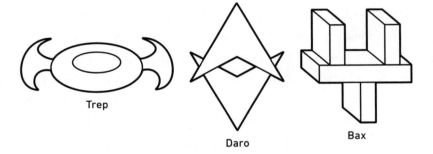

Trep

Daro

Bax

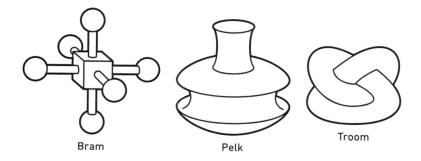

Bram

Pelk

Troom

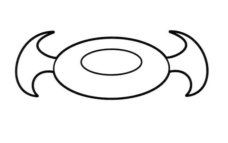

SYMBOLS CRASH

Scene 1

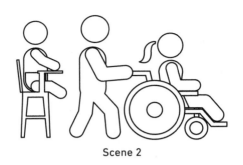

Scene 2

Scene 3

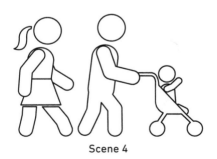

Scene 4

PAW PRESENCE

THE CURSE OF KNOWLEDGE

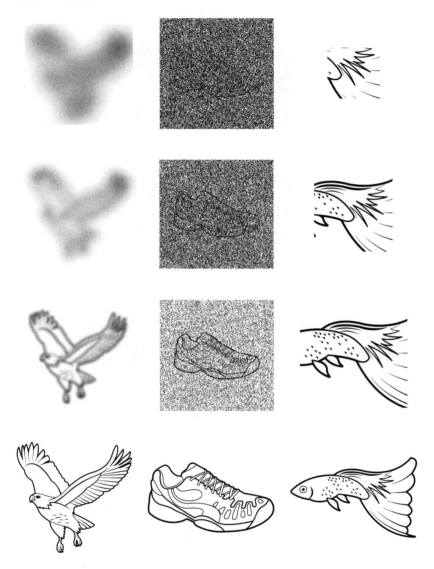

A STRANGE SORT

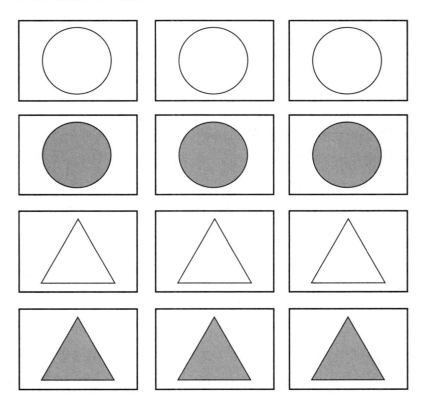

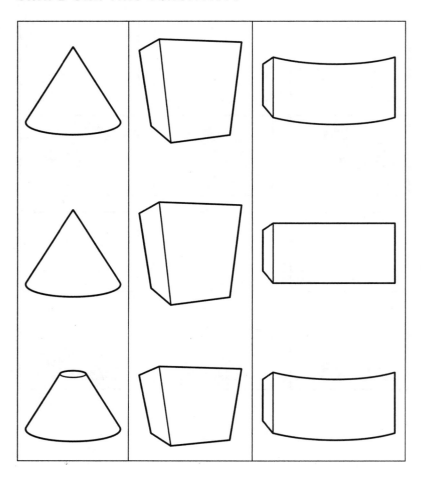

THE PLAYGROUND JUDGE

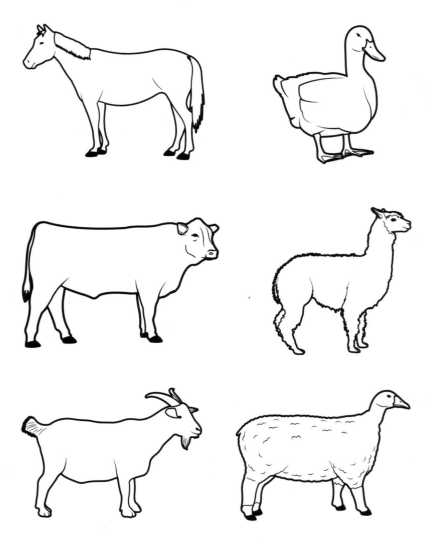

PROJECTS BY PRIMARY
RESEARCH AREA

COGNITIVE DEVELOPMENT
Sticking Around
Winners, More or Less
Bad Liars
Affirming Actions
Less Is More
The Curse of Knowledge
A Strange Sort
Tailored Teaching
Fishing for Prizes
Fantastic Work

DECISION MAKING
Pretzel Logic
Of Pigeons and Preschoolers

LANGUAGE DEVELOPMENT
Syntactic Sugar
Success Is Successive
Degrees of Distinction
The Effect of Causes
Symbols Crash
What Speaks Louder?
O, Really!

MEMORY AND ATTENTION
That's the Point
Focusing Exercise
Paw Presence
Working Memory Workout
Integrated Facts
The "Knew It All Along" Error
Absorption Awareness
Trying to Forget
A Light Wait

MOTIVATION
In the Groove
Leading Notes
The Batman Effect

MOTOR SKILLS
Sticking Around
Get a Grip

NUMBER SENSE
Impossible Adding
That Ain't Random
Bended Estimates

PERCEPTION
Artistic Intent
The Long and the Short
Wake or Sleep
Brain Blocks the Pain
Taught or Not
Shape-shifting Sensitivity

SOCIAL DEVELOPMENT
Wake or Sleep
First Dibs
Majority Rulers
What Speaks Louder?
On Premises
Dubious Advice
Who Knows Best?
Share What's Fair
The Playground Judge
Know Your Audience
No Sway

REFERENCES

IN THE GROOVE

Csikszentmihalyi, Mihaly. *Finding Flow: The Psychology of Engagement with Everyday Life*. New York: Basic Books, 1997.

Custodero, Lori A. "Observable Indicators of Flow Experience: A Developmental Perspective on Musical Engagement in Young Children from Infancy to School Age." *Music Education Research* 7, no. 2 (2005): 185–209.

IMPOSSIBLE ADDING

Lubin, Amélie, Sandrine Rossi, Nicolas Poirel, Céline Lanoë, Arlette Pineau, and Olivier Houdé. "The Role of Self-Action in 2-Year-Old Children: An Illustration of the Arithmetical Inversion Principle Before Formal Schooling." *Child Development Research* 2015 (2015).

SYNTACTIC SUGAR

Yuan, Sylvia, and Cynthia Fisher. "'Really? She Blicked the Baby?' Two-Year-Olds Learn Combinatorial Facts About Verbs by Listening." *Psychological Science* 20, no. 5 (2009): 619–26.

BOX: THE 30-MILLION-WORD GAP

Golinkoff, Roberta Michnick, Erika Hoff, Meredith L. Rowe, Catherine S. Tamis-LeMonda, and Kathy Hirsh-Pasek. "Language Matters: Denying the Existence of the 30-Million-Word Gap Has Serious Consequences." *Child Development* 90, no. 3 (2019): 985–92.

Hart, Betty, and Todd R. Risley. *Meaningful Differences in the Everyday Experience of Young American Children*. Baltimore: Paul H. Brookes, 1995.

Sperry, Douglas E., Linda L. Sperry, and Peggy J. Miller. "Reexamining the Verbal Environments of Children from Different Socioeconomic Backgrounds." *Child Development* 90, no. 4 (2019): 1303–18.

ARTISTIC INTENT

Preissler, Melissa Allen, and Paul Bloom. "Two-Year-Olds Use Artist Intention to Understand Drawings." *Cognition* 106, no. 1 (2008): 512–8.

Richert, R. A., and A. S. Lillard. "Children's Understanding of the Knowledge Prerequisites of Drawing and Pretending." *Developmental Psychology* 38, no. 6 (2002): 1004–15.

STICKING AROUND

Cox, Ralf F., and A. W. Smitsman. "Action Planning in Young Children's Tool Use." *Developmental Science* 9, no. 6 (2006): 628–41.

WINNERS, MORE OR LESS

Brannon, Elizabeth M., and Gretchen A. Van de Walle. "The Development of Ordinal Numerical Competence in Young Children." *Cognitive Psychology* 43, no. 1 (2001): 53–81.

BOX: PRESCHOOL PAIN SCALES

Von Baeyer, Carl L., Christine T. Chambers, Sasha J. Forsyth, Samantha Eisen, and Jennifer A. Parker. "Developmental Data Supporting Simplification of Self-report Pain Scales for Preschool-Age Children." *Journal of Pain* 14, no. 10 (2013): 1116–21.

Von Baeyer, Carl L., Lindsay S. Uman, Christine T. Chambers, and Adele Gouthro. "Can We Screen Young Children for Their Ability to Provide Accurate Self-reports of Pain?" *Pain* 152, no. 6 (2011): 1327–33.

BAD LIARS

Bender, Jasmine, Alison M. O'Connor, and Angela D. Evans. "Mirror, Mirror on the Wall: Increasing Young Children's Honesty Through Inducing Self-awareness." *Journal of Experimental Child Psychology* 167 (2018): 414–22.

Evans, Angela D., and Kang Lee. "Emergence of Lying in Very Young Children." *Developmental Psychology* 49, no. 10 (2013): 1958–63.

SUCCESS IS SUCCESSIVE

Schwab, Jessica F., and Casey Lew-Williams. "Repetition Across Successive Sentences Facilitates Young Children's Word Learning." *Developmental Psychology* 52, no. 6 (2016): 879–86.

THE LONG AND THE SHORT

Karg, Katja, Martin Schmelz, Josep Call, and Michael Tomasello. "All Great Ape Species (*Gorilla gorilla, Pan paniscus, Pan troglodytes, Pongo abelii*) and Two-and-a-Half-Year-Old Children (*Homo sapiens*) Discriminate Appearance from Reality." *Journal of Comparative Psychology* 128, no. 4 (2014): 431–9.

WAKE OR SLEEP

Williamson, Rebecca A., Rechele Brooks, and Andrew N. Meltzoff. "The Sound of Social Cognition: Toddlers' Understanding of How Sound Influences Others." *Journal of Cognition and Development* 16, no. 2 (2015): 252–60.

THAT'S THE POINT

Delgado, Begoña, Juan Carlos Gómez, and Encarnación Sarriá. "Pointing Gestures as a Cognitive Tool in Young Children: Experimental Evidence." *Journal of Experimental Child Psychology* 110, no. 3 (2011): 299–312.

LEADING NOTES

Koops, Lisa Huisman. "'Now Can I Watch My Video?': Exploring Musical Play Through Video Sharing and Social Networking in an Early Childhood Music Class." *Research Studies in Music Education* 34, no. 1 (2012): 15–28.

Suthers, L., and Amanda Niland. "An Exploration of Young Children's Engagement with Music Experiences." In *Listen to Their Voices: Research and Practice in Early*

Childhood Music, edited by Katharine Smithrim and Rena Upitis (Waterloo, Ontario: Canadian Music Educators' Association, 2007), 19–32.

BOX: MOBILE MELODIES

Koops, Lisa Huisman. "Songs from the Car Seat: Exploring the Early Childhood Music-Making Place of the Family Vehicle." *Journal of Research in Music Education* 62, no. 1 (2014): 52–65.

DEGREES OF DISTINCTION

Matthews, Danielle, Jessica Butcher, Elena Lieven, and Michael Tomasello. "Two- and Four-Year-Olds Learn to Adapt Referring Expressions to Context: Effects of Distracters and Feedback on Referential Communication." *Topics in Cognitive Science* 4, no. 2 (2012): 184–210.

AFFIRMING ACTIONS

Fritzley, V. Heather, Rod C. L. Lindsay, and Kang Lee. "Young Children's Response Tendencies Toward Yes-No Questions Concerning Actions." *Child Development* 84, no. 2 (2013): 711–25.

Lindberg, Marc A., Mary Tantalo Chapman, David Samsock, Stuart W. Thomas, and Anders W. Lindberg. "Comparisons of Three Different Investigative Interview Techniques with Young Children." *Journal of Genetic Psychology* 164, no. 1 (2003): 5–28.

Yuille, J. C., R. Hunter, R. Joffe, and J. Zaparniuk. "Interviewing Children in Sexual Abuse Cases." In *Child Victims, Child Witnesses*, edited by G. S. Goodman and B. L. Bottoms (New York: Guilford Press, 1993), 95–115.

FIRST DIBS

Friedman, Ori. "First Possession: An Assumption Guiding Inferences About Who Owns What." *Psychonomic Bulletin & Review* 15, no. 2 (2008): 290–5.

Friedman, Ori, and Karen R. Neary. "Determining Who Owns What: Do Children Infer Ownership from First Possession?" *Cognition* 107, no. 3 (2008): 829–49.

BOX: WORK TO OWN

Kanngiesser, Patricia, Nathalia Gjersoe, and Bruce M. Hood. "The Effect of Creative Labor on Property-Ownership Transfer by Preschool Children and Adults." *Psychological Science* 21, no. 9 (2010): 1236–41.

THE EFFECT OF CAUSES

Booth, Amy E. "Causal Supports for Early Word Learning." *Child Development* 80, no. 4 (2009): 1243–50.

SYMBOLS CRASH

Sutton, Ann, Natacha Trudeau, Jill Morford, Monica Rios, and Marie-Andrée Poirier. "Preschool-Aged Children Have Difficulty Constructing and Interpreting Simple Utterances Composed of Graphic Symbols." *Journal of Child Language* 37, no. 1 (2010): 1–26.

Trudeau, Natacha, Ann Sutton, Emmanuelle Dagenais, Sophie de Broeck, and Jill P. Morford. "Construction of Graphic Symbol Utterances by Children, Teenagers, and Adults: The Effect of Structure and Task Demands." *Journal of Speech, Language, and Hearing Research* 50, no. 5 (2007): 1314–29.

LESS IS MORE

Boysen, Sarah T., G. G. Bernston, M. B. Hannan, and J. T. Cacioppo. "Quantity-Based Interference and Symbolic Representations in Chimpanzees (Pan troglodytes)." *Journal of Experimental Psychology: Animal Behavior Processes* 22, no. 1 (1996): 76–86.

Carlson, Stephanie M., Angela C. Davis, and Jamie G. Leach. "Less Is More: Executive Function and Symbolic Representation in Preschool Children." *Psychological Science* 16, no. 8 (2005): 609–16.

MAJORITY RULERS

Corriveau, Kathleen H., and Paul L. Harris. "Preschoolers (Sometimes) Defer to the Majority in Making Simple Perceptual Judgments." *Developmental Psychology* 46, no. 2 (2010): 437–45.

BOX: ABANDONING THE PACK

Wilks, Matti, Emma Collier-Baker, and Mark Nielsen. "Preschool Children Favor Copying a Successful Individual over an Unsuccessful Group." *Developmental Science* 18, no. 6 (2015): 1014–24.

WHAT SPEAKS LOUDER?

Eskritt, Michelle, and Kang Lee. "Do Actions Speak Louder Than Words? Preschool Children's Use of the Verbal-Nonverbal Consistency Principle During Inconsistent Communications." *Journal of Nonverbal Behavior* 27, no. 1 (2003): 25–41.

Friend, Margaret. "The Transition from Affective to Linguistic Meaning." *First Language* 21, no. 63 (2001): 219–43.

FOCUSING EXERCISE

Budde, Henning, Claudia Voelcker-Rehage, Sascha Pietrabyk-Kendziorra, Pedro Ribeiro, and Günter Tidow. "Acute Coordinative Exercise Improves Attentional Performance in Adolescents." *Neuroscience Letters* 441, no. 2 (2008): 219–23.

Palmer, Kara K., Matthew W. Miller, and Leah E. Robinson. "Acute Exercise Enhances Preschoolers' Ability to Sustain Attention." *Journal of Sport and Exercise Psychology* 35, no. 4 (2012): 433–7.

PAW PRESENCE

Gee, Nancy R., Elise N. Crist, and Daniel N. Carr. "Preschool Children Require Fewer Instructional Prompts to Perform a Memory Task in the Presence of a Dog." *Anthrozoös* 23, no. 2 (2010): 173–84.

Gee, Nancy R., Jared K. Gould, Chad C. Swanson, and Ashley K. Wagner. "Preschoolers Categorize Animate Objects Better in the Presence of a Dog." *Anthrozoös* 25, no. 2 (2012): 187–98.

ON PREMISES

Köymen, Bahar, Maria Mammen, and Michael Tomasello. "Preschoolers Use Common Ground in Their Justificatory Reasoning with Peers." *Developmental Psychology* 52, no. 3 (2016): 423–9.

BOX: MORAL APPEALS

Mammen, Maria, Bahar Köymen, and Michael Tomasello. "The Reasons Young Children Give to Peers When Explaining Their Judgments of Moral and Conventional Rules." *Developmental Psychology* 54, no. 2 (2018): 254–62.

DUBIOUS ADVICE

Vanderbilt, Kimberly E., David Liu, and Gail D. Heyman. "The Development of Distrust." *Child Development* 82, no. 5 (2011): 1372–80.

THE CURSE OF KNOWLEDGE

Bernstein, Daniel M., Cristina Atance, Geoffrey Loftus, and Andrew N Meltzoff. "We Saw It All Along: Visual Hindsight Bias in Children and Adults." *Psychological Science* 15, no. 4 (2004): 264–7.

Birch, Susan A. J., Patricia Brosseau-Liard, Taeh Haddock, and Siba Ghrear. "A 'Curse of Knowledge' in the Absence of Knowledge? People Misattribute Fluency When Judging How Common Knowledge Is Among Their Peers." *Cognition* 166 (2017): 447–58.

THAT AIN'T RANDOM

Kushnir, Tamar, Fei Xu, and Henry M. Wellman. "Young Children Use Statistical Sampling to Infer the Preferences of Other People." *Psychological Science* 21, no. 8 (2010): 1134–40.

BRAIN BLOCKS THE PAIN

Dahlquist, Lynnda M., Kristine D. McKenna, Katia K. Jones, and Lindsay Dillinger. "Active and Passive Distraction Using a Head-Mounted Display Helmet: Effects on Cold Pressor Pain in Children." *Health Psychology* 26, no. 6 (2007): 794–801.

Weiss, Karen E., Lynnda M. Dahlquist, and Karen Wohlheiter. "The Effects of Interactive and Passive Distraction on Cold Pressor Pain in Preschool-Aged Children." *Journal of Pediatric Psychology* 36, no. 7 (2011): 816–26.

A STRANGE SORT

Bohlmann, Natalie L., and Larry Fenson. "The Effects of Feedback on Perseverative Errors in Preschool Aged Children." *Journal of Cognition and Development* 6, no. 1 (2005): 119–31.

WHO KNOWS BEST?

Bascandziev, Igor, and Paul L. Harris. "In Beauty We Trust: Children Prefer Information from More Attractive Informants." *British Journal of Developmental Psychology* 32, no. 1 (2014): 94–9.

Lane, Jonathan D., Henry M. Wellman, and Susan A. Gelman. "Informants' Traits Weigh Heavily in Young Children's Trust in Testimony and in Their Epistemic Inferences." *Child Development* 84, no. 4 (2013): 1253–68.

PRETZEL LOGIC

Atance, Cristina M., and Andrew N. Meltzoff. "Preschoolers' Current Desires Warp Their Choices for the Future." *Psychological Science* 17, no. 7 (2006): 583–7.

SHARE WHAT'S FAIR

Paulus, Markus, Samantha Gillis, Joyce Li, and Chris Moore. "Preschool Children Involve a Third Party in a Dyadic Sharing Situation Based on Fairness." *Journal of Experimental Child Psychology* 116, no. 1 (2013): 78–85.

O, REALLY!

Puranik, Cynthia S., and Christopher J. Lonigan. "From Scribbles to Scrabble: Preschool Children's Developing Knowledge of Written Language." *Reading and Writing* 24, no. 5 (2011): 567–89.

Puranik, Cynthia S., and Christopher J. Lonigan. "Name-Writing Proficiency, Not Length of Name, Is Associated with Preschool Children's Emergent Literacy Skills." *Early Childhood Research Quarterly* 27, no. 2 (2012): 284–94.

Welsch, Jodi G., Amie Sullivan, and Laura M. Justice. "That's My Letter!: What Preschoolers' Name Writing Representations Tell Us About Emergent Literacy Knowledge." *Journal of Literacy Research* 35, no. 2 (2003): 757–76.

TAUGHT OR NOT

Ziv, Margalit, Ayelet Solomon, and Douglas Frye. "Young Children's Recognition of the Intentionality of Teaching." *Child Development* 79, no. 5 (2008): 1237–56.

GET A GRIP

Weigelt, Matthias, and Thomas Schack. "The Development of End-State Comfort Planning in Preschool Children." *Experimental Psychology* 57, no. 6 (2010): 476–82.

BOX: SHELVING IT

Cohen, Rajal G., and David A. Rosenbaum. "Where Grasps Are Made Reveals How Grasps Are Planned: Generation and Recall of Motor Plans." *Experimental Brain Research* 157, no. 4 (2004): 486–95.

Jovanovic, Bianca, and Gudrun Schwarzer. "The Development of the Grasp Height Effect as a Measure of Efficient Action Planning in Children." *Journal of Experimental Child Psychology* 153 (2017): 74–82.

TAILORED TEACHING

Ronfard, Samuel, and Kathleen H. Corriveau. "Teaching and Preschoolers' Ability to Infer Knowledge from Mistakes." *Journal of Experimental Child Psychology* 150 (2016): 87–98.

FISHING FOR PRIZES

Beck, Sarah R., Ian A. Apperly, Jackie Chappell, Carlie Guthrie, and Nicola Cutting. "Making Tools Isn't Child's Play." *Cognition* 119, no. 2 (2011): 301–6.

OF PIGEONS AND PRESCHOOLERS

Mazur, James E., and Patricia E. Kahlbaugh. "Choice Behavior of Pigeons (*Columba livia*), College Students, and Preschool Children (*Homo sapiens*) in the Monty Hall Dilemma." *Journal of Comparative Psychology* 126, no. 4 (2012): 407–20.

BOX: MONKEYS ON MONTY

Klein, Emily D., Theodore Evans, Natasha B. Schultz, and Michael J. Beran. "Learning How to 'Make a Deal': Human (*Homo sapiens*) and Monkey (*Macaca mulatta*) Performance When Repeatedly Faced with the Monty Hall Dilemma." *Journal of Comparative Psychology* 127, no. 1 (2013): 103–8.

SHAPE-SHIFTING SENSITIVITY

Amir, Ori, Irving Biederman, Sarah B. Herald, Manan Shah, and Toben H. Mintz. "Greater Sensitivity to Nonaccidental Than Metric Shape Properties in Preschool Children." *Vision Research* 97, no. 10 (2014): 83–8.

WORKING MEMORY WORKOUT

Blakey, Emma, and Daniel J. Carroll. "A Short Executive Function Training Program Improves Preschoolers' Working Memory." *Frontiers in Psychology* 6 (2015): 1827.

INTEGRATED FACTS

Varga, Nicole L., Rebekah A. Stewart, and Patricia J. Bauer. "Integrating Across Episodes: Investigating the Long-term Accessibility of Self-Derived Knowledge in 4-Year-Old Children." *Journal of Experimental Child Psychology* 145 (2016): 48–63.

THE PLAYGROUND JUDGE

Smetana, Judith G., Nicole Campione-Barr, and Nicole Yell. "Children's Moral and Affective Judgments Regarding Provocation and Retaliation." *Merrill-Palmer Quarterly* 49, no. 2 (2003): 209–36.

THE "KNEW IT ALL ALONG" ERROR

Cimpian, Andrei, and Lucy C. Erickson. "Remembering Kinds: New Evidence That Categories Are Privileged in Children's Thinking." *Cognitive Psychology* 64, no. 3 (2012): 161–85.

Sutherland, Shelbie L., and Andrei Cimpian. "Children Show Heightened Knew-It-All-Along Errors When Learning New Facts About Kinds: Evidence for the Power of Kind Representations in Children's Thinking." *Developmental Psychology* 51, no. 8 (2015): 1115–30.

BENDED ESTIMATES

Berteletti, Ilaria, Daniela Lucangeli, Manuela Piazza, Stanislas Dehaene, and Marco Zorzi. "Numerical Estimation in Preschoolers." *Developmental Psychology* 46, no. 2 (2010): 545–51.

Feigenson, Lisa, Stanislas Dehaene, and Elizabeth Spelke. "Core Systems of Number." *Trends in Cognitive Sciences* 8, no. 7 (2004): 307–14.

ABSORPTION AWARENESS

Lipowski, Stacy L., William E. Merriman, and John Dunlosky. "Preschoolers Can Make Highly Accurate Judgments of Learning." *Developmental Psychology* 49, no. 8 (2013): 1505–16.

BOX: JUDGMENT HELPS

Janes, Jessica L., Michelle L. Rivers, and John Dunlosky. "The Influence of Making Judgments of Learning on Memory Performance: Positive, Negative, or Both?" *Psychonomic Bulletin & Review* 25, no. 6 (2018): 2356–64.

Soderstrom, Nicholas C., Colin T. Clark, Vered Halamish, and Elizabeth Bjork. "Judgments of Learning as Memory Modifiers." *Journal of Experimental Psychology: Learning, Memory, and Cognition* 41, no. 2 (2015): 553–8.

THE BATMAN EFFECT

White, Rachel E., Emily O. Prager, Catherine Schaefer, Ethan Kross, Angela Duckworth, and Stephanie M. Carlson. "The 'Batman Effect': Improving Perseverance in Young Children." *Child Development* 88, no. 5 (2017): 1563–71.

KNOW YOUR AUDIENCE

Baer, Carolyn, and Ori Friedman. "Fitting the Message to the Listener: Children Selectively Mention General and Specific Facts." *Child Development* 89, no. 2 (2018): 461–75.

FANTASTIC WORK

Pierucci, Jillian M., Christopher T. O'Brien, Melissa McInnis Brown, Ansley Gilpin, and Angela Barber. "Fantasy Orientation Constructs and Related Executive Function Development in Preschool: Developmental Benefits to Executive Functions by Being a Fantasy-Oriented Child." *International Journal of Behavioral Development* 38, no. 1 (2013): 62–9.

BOX: FANTASY CAMP

Thibodeau, Rachel B., Ansley T. Gilpin, Melissa M. Brown, and Brooke A. Meyer. "The Effects of Fantastical Pretend-Play on the Development of Executive Functions: An Intervention Study." *Journal of Experimental Child Psychology* 145 (2016): 120–38.

TRYING TO FORGET

Hupbach, Almut, Jenny L. Weinberg, and Victoria L. Shiebler. "Forget-Me, Forget-Me-Not: Evidence for Directed Forgetting in Preschoolers." *Cognitive Development* 45 (2018): 24–30.

Nietzsche, Friedrich. *On the Advantage and Disadvantage of History for Life.* Translated by Peter Preuss. Indianapolis: Hackett, 1980.

NO SWAY

De Neys, Wim, and Karolien Vanderputte. "When Less Is Not Always More: Stereotype Knowledge and Reasoning Development." *Developmental Psychology* 47, no. 2 (2011): 432.

A LIGHT WAIT

Correa-Chávez, Maricela, and Barbara Rogoff. "Children's Attention to Interactions Directed to Others: Guatemalan Mayan and European American Patterns." *Developmental Psychology* 45, no. 3 (2009): 630–41.

Acknowledgments

Many thanks to my editors, Lauren Appleton and Marian Lizzi; my agent, Laurie Abkemeier; and everyone at Penguin Random House who helped make this book happen.

I am also grateful for the love and support of my wife, Tanya; my children, Joel, Benjamin, and Grace (on whom I've performed many of these experiments); my parents, Frank and Betty; and other family members and friends who have helped and encouraged me along the way.

About the Author

Shaun Gallagher, a former magazine and newspaper editor, now writes books and software. He lives with his wife and children in northern Delaware.

His other books are:

- *Experimenting with Babies: 50 Amazing Science Projects You Can Perform on Your Kid* (experimentingwithbabies.com)

- *Experiments for Newlyweds: 50 Amazing Science Projects You Can Perform with Your Spouse* (newlywed.science)

- *Correlated: Surprising Connections Between Seemingly Unrelated Things* (correlated.org)

Also by SHAUN GALLAGHER

EXPERIMENTING with **BABIES**

50 Amazing Science Projects You Can Perform on Your Kid

Shaun Gallagher

"*Experimenting with Babies* is a wonderful book, giving parents a hands-on way to understand their baby's emerging mind. What a fabulous way for parents to get to know their new child!"

—LISE ELIOT, Ph.D., author of *What's Going On in There? How the Brain and Mind Develop in the First Five Years of Life*

tarcherperigee